ANGLICANIA:

OR,

ENGLAND'S MISSION

TO THE CELT.

BY

J. BIRMINGHAM.

LONDON:
THOMAS RICHARDSON AND SON,
26, PATERNOSTER ROW;
9, CAPEL STREET, DUBLIN; AND DERBY.
MDCCCLXIII.

PREFACE.

The performances of England's mission to up-
root Catholicity among the Irish, and the charac-
teristics of Anglican doctrine, which I venture to
comprise in the general name of *Anglicania,* do
not present a promising theme for successful treatment in rhyme. On the contrary, the materials
they furnish to a writer must be considered as
eminently prosaic, or at least unfit for *serious*
verse, and when I began the present composition
it was with an attempt at a humorous and ironic
strain. However, without well knowing how I
was led to the change, I soon found myself inclining to an opposite style, in which I went on
versifying to an extent that I had little antici-
pated; and the production contains few traces of
my original design, except in some lines in the
commencement. To relieve the ungenial nature
of the subject, I have introduced matter which,
I hope, may, in some degree, have that effect
without being considered altogether episodical;
and that my book should not show complete

dryness as a metrical performance would, in one point of view, be the highest success which I could reasonably expect to attain.

Certainly, in addressing our *Anglican Missionaries*, I did not at first intend to introduce any discussion of their doctrines, as my object was to show the viciousness of their preaching rather than the errors of what they preached; and I wished to avoid giving any semblance of offence to that great proportion of Protestants, whose Christianity appears unfeigned in its quietness, and whose convictions I respect as sincere. However, after further consideration, I decided on adverting to some of the more prominent difficulties in the religion to which the *missionaries* would attract us; as I thought it right to show how hopeless must be their task of conversion where those objections to their creed were so plainly to be seen. I also considered it proper to indicate the undoubted fact, that *if they could* persuade us to look less favourably on our old religion, we should yet *not be attracted to theirs;* for, with such visible defects in Reformed Doctrine, their strictures on Catholic Belief, if they had any weight, would lead not to Anglicanism but to infidelity.

Still, in my remarks on Anglican tenets, I do not aim at that species of controversy which I think scarcely at all allowable in verse, and not well adapted to the pen of a layman. My design is not to argue, on Scriptural grounds, any Sacramental Doctrine, but rather to point out to Anglicans their simultaneous assertions and denials of certain principles; and in directing attention to contradictions in a faith I do not feel that I am trenching upon the province of a theologian. Further, I wish it to be distinctly understood, that when I use any severities of language against Anglicanism, I regard it in its character of an *aggressive institution ;* and it is in consideration of its efforts to *uncatholicize* Ireland, and *for the purpose of showing how it encourages us to conversion,* that I think it right to set forth its effects, not alone *here,* but *at home* in England; and with the same object I refer to the part that it has lately played on the occasion of the Indian mutiny. With the religion of Anglicans, indeed, as far as it relates only to themselves, I would not quarrel; but when I observe it in its hostility to mine, and in its effects on my country, in its proselyting attempts and political feats, I think myself entitled to explain how slight must be its claims to our admiration.

The results of its *missionary* career amongst us are but too palpable : they are the plunder of our

property and the immolation of our race; and not
to hate the "*Establishment*" we must close our
ears to its voice and shut our eyes to its acts.
From the butcheries of Elizabeth and Cromwell
down to the last eviction of the scrupulous Catholic tenant, its deeds in this island have been an-
tagonistic to all that the human mind can consider
good.   Though the spilling of our blood is not
now within its legal power, the law between landlord and tenant still brings it victims indirectly;
and, no longer allowed to follow with fire and
sword, it yet pursues with abuse and falsehood.
The Anglican Press teems with slander of Catholicity; the pulpit bellows forth its unceasing libel;
and the plundered edifice, that was consecrated for
the worship of God, now resounds with the vitu-
peration of those by whose piety it was erected.
Not content with this, the missionaries placard
their insults on our walls; and they may be
tracked over the country, where the highways are
strewed with publications abusive of our religion
and impious with citations of the Sacred Writings.

Thus ever changeless in its persecuting spirit,
the MISSION offends where it fails to convert, and,
in addition, oppresses when it can.   It is not long
since one of its chief dignitaries caused the hills
of a remote district to re-echo with the cries

of whole families unhoused in a most severe winter. Yet with the wails of those people ringing in our ears, and with the affronts of the MISSION ever flung in our faces, we are still "*affectionately invited*" (as the phrase goes) to join its saintly fold. Harassing a people, befooling its supporters, and desecrating the name of Religion, it deserves little forbearance from him who makes it the subject of his censure; and surely no one of Christian feeling and ordinary discernment will blame the reviewer of its proceedings for any hard words that he may use against it.

One might naturally be surprised at the perseverance in a system which is contrary to everything that could give a hope of success; but perhaps it secures the result that is *really intended;* and the noisy libels and the bustling abuse that fail to make proselytes, may yet ensure the maintenance of the *preaching staff.* We can conceive how those who hear the din of assault at a distance may be persuaded that it prospers; and it is possible that the loud fury of the MISSION achieves its true object while it keeps the hopes of *Exeter Hall* alive, and stimulates the untying of its purse-strings. Many will accept this surmise as the most probable explanation of a zeal so opposed in character to its pretended source; and there is, doubtless, some difficulty in understanding how they, who are so clever in collecting the *supplies*, could, at the same time, be so foolish as to expect their utility for the purpose intended by the donors.

To be seduced from our belief, we should, indeed, perceive allurements other than those that are presented by the preachers who would convert us. The abuse of our Catholic Faith tends little to the advantage of that which possesses not a feature by which the Church of Christ may be known. It is of no avail to *assume* the name of *Catholic* in opposition to the Creed whose unity is recognised over the earth; or to offer, for our preference, that diverse doctrine, whose pretended universality, like that of Isis, would have a variegated robe for its type, rather than the simple seamless coat of the Saviour.* We must, therefore, remain attached to the religion in whose oneness we behold a standing miracle to prove its Heavenly origin; and whose Catholicity is plainly that which the Scripture has promised—attracting without violence, and expanding without segregation.

Conceived in anger, established here by vice,

* St. Cyprian in his book on *Unity*, speaks of the seamless coat of our Saviour, as signifying the unity of His Church.

and perpetuated by a secular institution, Reformed Doctrine cannot appear very inviting to us, who see its working at the present day, and are not ignorant of its history. An unsound fragment, splitting from the rock of our Communion not to rise, but to fall, and further splitting as it falls, it attracts us not in its course of ruin.

That Anglicanism is not, indeed, gaining ground among the Irish, has been clearly demonstrated by the last census. Elate with the expected results of famine and extermination, the friends of the MIS-SION had been loudly boasting that the census of 1861 would prove an approaching equality of numbers in our Catholic and non-Catholic population. Their hopes were not realized; for, in spite of the enormous losses on the side of the Catholics, the ratio of their excess was but very slightly diminished. Notwithstanding local descents, the general route may be upwards; and the checks from physical causes in disastrous years do not prevent Catholicity from showing a large increase in Ireland since the first authentic reports. It appears that in 1733, Catholics were to Protestants as 8 to 3,* while the late census gives the ratio of $10\frac{2}{3}$ to 3. In Mayo, one of the

* See an excellent article on the "State of the Irish Church" in Edin. Review of July 1835.

chief "fields of labor" of the *Missionaries*,
we find an eminent proof of the futility of their
efforts and the falseness of their boastful assertions.　Here there were not more than 12
Catholics to 1 Protestant (according to the Report
of a Parliamentary Committee) in 1731, but the
proportion of the former to the latter was as 30
to 1 in 1834, and it was within a small fraction
of the same in 1861; though nowhere else did
extermination and famine perhaps so thoroughly
combine to reduce the numbers of the Catholics,
and though we give credit to the Protestants for
every non-Catholic denomination and *every person* whose creed was *not distinctly ascertained.*
In certain districts of Mayo and Galway, there
has been an increase of Protestants, caused by
the immigration of strangers.　That the MIS-
SION in those parts can claim some conversions
also, is freely admitted; but their *value* to its
cause may be inferred from the following:—in
the case of the Rev. George Shea against the
Rev. Thos. Ronayne, tried at the Clifden Sessions
in July 1860, a Bible-reader swore that he always
intended to have *the priest* at the hour of his
death, and, though preaching to make converts to
the MISSION for the purpose of earning his bread,
he never ceased to be a Roman Catholic in his

heart. I have the best authorities for this evidence, and, among them, the chairman of the court. Another Bible-reader in the same district, who was attached to the MISSION for 14 years, believing himself to be in danger of death, sent for the priest, the Rev. T. Ronayne. This gentleman succeeded, by the aid of an escort of police, in penetrating to the chamber of the sick man, who admitted that his heart was never with those whom he had been serving for so long a period. Other similar cases could be cited, but the above will suffice. No more than the Catholic, will any sincere Protestant regret the fewness of those conversions when he is made aware of their character; nor will the pious stranger, after his tour of inspection, be edified when he discovers that he had been duped into the belief of *missionary* success by the trick of filling the churches on his route with a *mobilised* congregation.

The poverty and sufferings of Ireland are made the subject of taunt by the Anglicans. They make us poor; and blame us for being so. It would be a task rather of long labor than difficulty to show all the overwhelming advantages given at every period, even since the great persecution, to England over this country both by Parliament and Executive; but it is one that need not be per-

formed when we find in a single cause sufficient
grounds for charging the crime of our poverty on
Anglican institutions. We cannot expect a peasantry to be very prosperous, whose labors go
solely to enrich others, and who, after the toil of
years, find the fruits of their industry snatched
out of their hands, and themselves turned adrift
on the world. It is this peasantry who are so
abused for being poor, and, as it is maintained,
ignorant; and by those, too, who would forbid
their becoming independent, and would deny them
an education that they could conscientiously
accept. Still their oppressors, triumphantly flour-
ishing the Bible, proclaim, that their poverty is
the punishment of God for their religion. It may,
indeed, be the chastening of God for faults in their
observance of it; but if those who so exhort from
the Bible, would not shut their own eyes to the
warnings it contains, they would see that the
enemies of the God of Israel were often made the
instruments wherewith he punished his own people.
They might advantageously reflect on the Egyp-
tian bondage, and might remember that if the
iniquity of the Amorites was full only after *four*
hundred years,* the sway of Anglicanism over
Ireland has as yet barely existed for *three*. They

* Gen. xiv, 13-16. Acts, vii, 6-7.

might also take into profitable consideration the
fact that, generally, the punisher of God's people
was, in the end, himself punished; nor ought
they let the fate of Pharaoh, Nebuchadnezzar,
Sennacherib, or the Amorites themselves, escape
their regard.

In conclusion, I may repeat my wish to draw a
clear distinction between our Anglican *Missionaries*
and those who, honestly dissenting from the Faith
of Catholics, still oppose it not in the spirit of insult
or oppression.   To Protestants of this class, lovers
of justice, there is, I hope, nothing offensive in
what I write; and my labor shall not be without
a good result if those of them who may chance to
read the following pages, may be induced, by the
facts which I notice, to reflect on the rise, progress, and present state of Reformed Doctrine,
into whose history they have, probably, not taken
pains to inquire.

                                        J. B.

January 1st, 1863.

ANGLICANIA.

—

PART I.

ANGLICANIA.

PART I.

When the Reformers, in a pious fright,
Found that the Spirit had withdrawn his light—
That Christ's assurance had completely failed,
While, signally, the gates of hell prevailed,[1]
They boldly then with holy zeal propounded,
To mend the unstable structure God had founded,
And preached the vainness of the hope sublime,
That He was with His Church, and for all time.[2]
   The good results of their divine ambition
Were many a new and oft-revised edition
Of Faith's old book, into whose pages crept
Errors, while Heaven, fatigued with watching, slept.
To spread the doctrine, in whose form appeared
True Christian faith from all those errors cleared,
Was next, of course, the right and anxious aim
Of each new rival in Reforming fame.
They thus, unwearied in the works of change,
Besought conversion in an ample range ;

---

(1) Matthew xvi. 18. (2) Id. xxviii. 20.

But yet, though many in its truth believed,
Reform was by most Christians unreceived;
And in its days of palmiest success
It seemed, indeed, even slower to progress
Than some old heresies of wider sway,
That smote the Church, but now are passed away.[3]
And hateful Rome still unreformed appears,
Despite the preachings of three hundred years.
Ours, like the Heathen's Heaven, seems ruled by
      Fate;
Or why Rome's blemishes perpetuate?
Yet some there are who do not yet despair
To pull the Pontiff from St. Peter's chair.
And England, whose true piety rejects
The rights of Pagans, and their Gods respects,[4]
Pursues, untired, her long laborious mission,
To win the West from Popery's perdition.
Many her zealous workers in the Fold;
Their faith made lively by the generous gold,
Subscribed in pitying fondness as the price
Of Erin's passage paid to Paradise.
Wondrous the treasure that from year to year
England expends upon her MISSION here!
To each chief saint a measure she confides,
Who, with much skill, among the saints divides:

(3) The Church was more shaken by Arianism than by any other
heresy.   Protestantism never attained to its importance.   St.
Jerome complained that the world was turning to it; yet, where is it
now?

(4) It will be easily understood that I allude principally to the
military honours paid by the British to *Juggernaut*, perhaps even
at the present, but certainly up to a recent period.

Proportioned well to holiness, no doubt,
Does he, of course the holiest, share it out.
The *working* saints, expounding o'er the land,
Toil on ; but little on their modest band
His prudent gospel spends ; and, rightly, these
Do all the sacred drudgery for low fees,
Visit each hut, and, of her wrath unwary,
Placard each challenge to the Virgin Mary.[5]

In ceaseless labor those good men appear
For love of Heaven and their pay per year ;
And it is curious to observe how each
Displays his own peculiar power to teach :
While some with saintly drawl, and tract in hand,
Preach to the stubborn peasants of our land ;
Others, the force of mild persuasion lacking,
Impress true Christian doctrine by *skull-cracking*,[6]

(5) The profits secured by the higher class of Saints are not made public; one of the inferior order swore at a trial at the assizes of Castlebar, that *his* salary was £3. a month.

(6) "*The skull-cracker*," a favourite instrument of physical argument used by the missionaries, consists of a heavy ball of lead attached to a cord of convenient length, and, when swung by the arm of an athletic saint, must prove very effective for the purpose intended. Firearms too are frequently carried.

It is not surprising that the warlike tendencies and moral behaviour of the *missionaries* should often cause their attendance at the criminal courts of law, as we see by the trials reported from time to time in the newspapers. It would not be edifying, nor is it necessary to give extracts from reported cases like one that was tried at the Ballinrobe Sessions of January 1852, for the purpose of showing the characters that are found among the holy confraternity, one of whom, at a more recent trial in Mayo, *swore* that he *was* a saint! I believe it was at the Petty Sessions Court in Tuam that the beauties of the " skull-cracker" were first explained.

To which bold system we may surely find
Reformers at all periods most inclined.
The ancient gentle type of Christian preaching
Appeared not fit for modern Christian teaching;
And if the *Faith* required a reformation,
Why not as well its *way of propagation ?*
Or a new method might we not concede
To preach what seems to many a new creed?
And must we marvel at the altered mode
By which Reformers judge the love of God,
When poverty, once thought no cursed sign,
They look on as a proof of wrath divine,
And equally believe that worldly wealth
Thrives in proportion to the spirit's health? [7]
    Yet with the marks of truth that it displays
The MISSION leads us not from Popish ways.
And now, adopting a more serious strain—
We ask, has time not proved its efforts vain ?
We love it not, whose dread historic page
Proves it our enemy in every age:
In its long rule dispensing all the woes
Its hate could fancy and its power impose :
The ceaseless purpose of its enterprise—
Or to extirpate or to barbarise,
And torture; for it spared but to oppress:
It plundered ; then forbade us to possess :

(7) In the English press we often find the poverty and sufferings of
Ireland attributed to the anger of the Almighty on account of her
steadfastness in her faith; the wealth and supremacy of England
being, on the other hand, esteemed a sign of God's favor to that
country. In the same way we must suppose that by the captivities
of the Jews the falsity of their belief and the truth of that of the
Egyptians or the Assyrians was signified.

Knowledge forbade—a crime to educate—
Learning's renowned old seats made desolate ;
While murderous gospel panted through the lands
For those " the Lord might yield into its hands."
 Midst ruin then this mission's teaching glowed,
And sparkled brightest upon streams of blood—
Blood of the people, and of priests even priced
For Moloch's altar in the name of Christ :
Priced to the hunter like destructive beasts :
Of equal value, heads of wolves and priests.
But at the gibbet that replaced the cross,
Or fleeing through the wood or mountain moss,
The Irish priest held to Religion true ;
And, like their priest, so held his people too.
Escaping from the temple overturned
Where incense to the God of peace had burned,
He called the God of martyrs down to bless
A lowly temple in the wilderness.
To him the cavern, as the catacomb,
To the old martyred saints of heathen Rome ; [8]

(8) Apocalypse xvii. 6, xviii. 24. I am not among those who consider Imperial Britain as the great Babylon of the Apocalypse ;
though it must be admitted that the points of resemblance are
striking. It little matters whether London is built on *seven hills*,
as some affirm, or not ; for the seven hills are distinctly called
seven kings (xvii. 9) as the *many waters*, on which Babylon sat, were
peoples and nations (ver. 1, 15) whom England, it might be asserted,
subdued to her empire. The chief similitude—and it is remarkable
—appears to me to exist in the great wealth derived from the com-
merce of a seafaring people ; of whom " *all were made rich that had
ships at sea*" (xviii. 19), and whose " *merchants were the great men of
the earth*" (ver. 23.) and over whom the merchants of the earth *shall
weep* (v. 11.) when the great city and her *riches come to nought, and
every shipmaster and all that sail into the lake* [q. *the river*] *and work*

Nor long secure was even this last defence
Against the untired hunter's diligence.
  Some blest retreat indeed we seek in vain
That saw no outrage of the MISSION'S reign.
From north to south, from east to west, we try,
But find not where the blood-pest did not lie :—
From Antrim's pillared coast, where wondrous
    forms
Of nature's sculpture meet the northern storms,
To Ros ui Carbre, or Dun Cearmna's height,
Whose cliffs the billow of the south invite.
Or from Imaile's vales and mountain shrines, [9]
From the wild lake that by the round tower shines,
Even to the farthest west beyond the tide
Of glorious Corrib's well-loved waters wide—
To where the earth, from her old fiery deeps,
Heaved up, in times untold, the granite heaps
That darkly rise, in many a heathered pile,
Over Moycullen, or around the isle
Of far Garomna, off the Coast of Bays,
Against the great Atlantic ramparts raise.
Yes! we may search our land from shore to shore,
Each plain survey, each hill, each vale, explore,

in the sea shall stand afar off." (v. 17.) The products of INDIA seem
to be plainly included in the 12th and 13th verses; and the conclusion of the latter reminds us strongly of the ANGLICAN MISSION. Is
it not strange that those who apply this description of wealthy
Babylon to _modern Rome_ at the same time insist on her unprosperous state, and pretend to sympathize with the wretchedness of
her people under the Papal Government ?

  (9) _Ros ui Carbre_; _Dun Cearmna_—ancient names of places on the
coast of Cork. _Imaile_—Wicklow.

Compass it all, and yet no place remains
Unsullied by this MISSION's murder-stains.[19]

(10) A few examples of its earlier endeavors will show how " the
MISSION" exerted itself, ever according to the means within its reach,
to *win the affections* of the Irish people. By an act of Elizabeth it
was made high treason to assert the *spiritual* supremacy of the Pope,
and by her command to Carew, the Deputy of Munster, her officers
were to "*put suspected Irish to the rack, and to torture them when
they should find it convenient.*" Never was an order better obeyed.
In the reign of Charles I. the Anglicans, getting exasperated at some
remission in the persecution of Catholics, published the following
manifesto, which appears in Plowden's History of Ireland (Appendix
vol. i. No. 18.) "*The religion of the Papists is superstitious and
idolatrous, their faith and doctrine erroneous and heretical, their
church, in respect of both, apostatical: to give them, therefore, toleration, or to consent that they may freely exercise their religion and profess their faith and doctrine, is a grievous sin, and that in two respects:
for first it is to make ourselves accessory not only to their superstitions,
idolatries, and heresies, and, in a word, to all the abominations of
Popery: but also, (which is a consequent of the former) to the perdition
of the seduced people which perish in the deluge of the Catholic apos-
tacy.*" The remainder of the manifesto alludes to a loyal offer made
by the grateful Catholics, and, after a touch of the usual blasphemous cant about the most *precious blood of our Saviour, and zeal for
God's glory,* exclaims against the offer in question being permitted
to induce any toleration of "*Popery, superstition, and idolatory.*" It is
signed by twelve archbishops and bishops, *Armagh* leading. By an
English statute of Elizabeth it is ordered that "*no Jesuit or popish
priest shall come into* OR BE *in the realm on pain of high treason unless he conform,*" (27 El. c. 2, s. 2, 3, 10.) *and if any person shall
knowingly receive or relieve any such he shall be guilty of felony
without benefit of clergy.*" (s. 4.) By the 7th W. III. and 8th Anne,
Irish statutes, education of papists either at home or abroad was
sought to be rendered *impossible.* By the 7th Will. III. c. 5, no
Papist was permitted to keep a horse which was valued so high as
five pounds. By the 2nd Anne, papist clergymen coming to Ireland
and officiating there were guilty of felony. By the 12th Geo. I. c. 3,
any popish priest or reputed popish priest, marrying two Protestants,
or a Protestant and a Papist, was made *guilty of felony without
benefit of clergy.*
    Cromwell, reporting his massacre of the capitulated garrison and

But as the MISSION more our land oppressed,
With Christian fortitude it seemed more blessed.
Religion trampled was not less of God,
And firmer grew as persecutors trod.
God never let the faith of Erin fade,
When, as a nation, even most decayed:
Then like the pine she stood, whose boughs are seen,
Withered next earth, while those next heaven are
     green.
     If now the MISSION's rage doth lighter press,
'Tis that its force, and not its hate is less.
Yet, though the conqueror's sword it may not draw,
It still gains victims by more quiet law.
The exiled thousands that our land outpours,
Each year unceasingly, to distant shores;
The lost that under the Atlantic lie,
Or they who starve, or in the pest house die:
These now are the chief victims it displays
In humbled power of less rampant days;
For scarce an ill that lays our country waste
But to this mission may be surely traced;

inhabitants of Drogheda, stated *that he did not leave thirty persons
alive in the town: that every faithful man should ascribe to God alone
the glory of the achievement which was a wonderful act of divine
mercy.* I believe it was on this occasion that he exclaimed, "*The
Lord hath delivered them into our hands,*" but his gospel feat at
Drogheda was far exceeded by his performances during the five
days' slaughter at Wexford, where 300 women were evangelically
put to death in one batch around the market cross. A proclamation,
signed by Chas. Fleetwood, Edmund Ludlow, and John Jones,
offered the *prize given for the head of a wolf, or £5. for every head of a
Catholic priest.* But all this apostolic fervor was in vain, and the
inflexible Irish still remained unconvinced of the divine truths of the
MISSION's teaching.

And all must own it the substantial cause
Of evils done by its supporting laws :
Not those which rule its points of faith indeed,
But those intended to impose its creed.
With their own ills those blighting laws pursue
And leave us liable to others too ;
For, though, in truth, they may not now oppress
As in old times of our complete distress,
And are so modified, that they appear
Of little note compared to what they were,
Yet the deplorable effect remains
Of long continued and excessive pains ;
And they have taken so our strength away,
That the poor country falls an easy prey
To every evil, come from whence it may.

Such are the consequences that appear
To prove the working of this MISSION here;
Whose hateful story of unceasing rage
It fain would hide beneath the Bible's page ;
And the low dreadful spirit it reveals
As zeal celestial to the world appeals ;
So earth's deep fires, through Cotopaxi riven,
Flame in the clouds, as if they came from heaven.

Weary and slow the steps by which we rose
To a less slavish state midst furious foes.
The highest point that we as yet have gained
Was by O'Connell's leadership attained.
Before his time a not less noble mind
Had the renowned achievement well designed.
Grattan, who once the pride of England broke,
From off the Catholic would lift the yoke :

Grattan, a Protestant, whose conscience blessed,
In him, the creed he honestly professed,
Sincere himself, would no oppressor be,
To punish others for sincerity.
But he survived not till the stronger strain
Of "the Emancipator" burst the chain.
He passed away: and generous Heaven decreed
A more illustrious quickly to succeed;
And, like a fire-ball in the morning sky,
That rushes to the brightening east to die,
'Twas in the rising of O'Connell's light
That Grattan disappeared from Erin's sight.
    Grattan, indeed, a noble conquest gained;
Though short the time that conquest was main-
    tained;
And the world saw in glorious "*eighty-two*"
How Protestants could turn to Erin true.
But brief was the success we then achieved,
And sad the independence we received,
Which only to be ruined was retrieved.
Grattan both saw our cradled freedom smile
And its dead body on the funeral pile.
So soon, alas, was victory undone
We may regret that it was ever won.
Yet if its deeds no more in brightness glow,
A majesty, though dimmed, they ever show.
The deep eclipse that o'er their splendor came
Has not displaced them from the heaven of fame.
As when, at even, on the west of red,
Outlined in gloom a mountain range is spread;
When peak and pinnacle display their height,
Like gaps of darkness in the narrowing light,

The shadowed earth still swells to brilliant
    skies,
Obscured, yet grand; and so our triumphs rise.
    But then O'Connell's conquests still remain,
Full bright; though traitors' acts oft make them
    vain.
To gain one greater still he only failed,
Because dissension's ancient curse prevailed.
Nor long, indeed, true patriotism survived,
When discord in its councils now arrived:
Well did this severed state its close portend,
As delta'd streams, dividing, mark their end.
    Yet shall O'Connell's fame for ever rest
Secure in every thoughtful Irish breast.
By peaceful struggles he would persevere,
And to that policy remained sincere.
By that he once succeeded, and believed
Our fortunes by it still were best retrieved.
Like the huge iceberg, that defies the storm,
He saw our sorrows rear a stubborn form.
When wrath assails they only greater grow,
Even as the Iceberg in the tempest's snow.
Yet, as the wintry mass dissolves away
In polar sunshine's mild unsetting ray,
He thought our grievances should yield at
    length
Surely to peaceful and untiring strength.
    But as O'Connell thus to peace adhered;
So was he by our foes disliked and feared,
Whose constant plan, the easier to oppress,
Would goad our land to acts of lawlessness.

By this proud Christian scheme their conquering
    hate
Crushed Erin low in fatal "*ninety-eight.*"
Then, as of old, their slaughter-lust ensnared
A thoughtless mob unguided, unprepared;
Though one small district, risen in wrath, alone,
Long shook their Moloch's deep-ensanguined
    throne.
O'Connell's wisdom and religious sense
Denied that lust a similar pretence;
And just for this his enemies appear
Still to malign his great and good career;
But yet, in spite of slander's poisoned darts,
His memory lives revered in Irish hearts:
Vain are the efforts of his various foes
In hate or envy: when they interpose
To darken his broad disk, their little spheres
But transits make, while no eclipse appears.

    And you, the MISSION's stern supporters here,
And whose support has ever made it clear,
That this dread MISSION with its reddened rod,
Is not *of* God, but is, *itself*, your god—
Adored, because all right it drives away,
And grants its votaries unrighteous sway—
You know that while we suffer wrongs from you,
Both parties suffer wrongs in common too:—
Such once were the foul laws that England
    made,
To check our industry, to cramp our trade;
And those she only ventured to impose,
Because she found in you your country's foes.

Those laws extinct, a system still remains
That our land's wealth away to England drains;
But, ever your ascendancy to save,
You bear all evils though you shout and rave,[11]
And, to support the loved *Establishment*,
That you may wrongs inflict, to wrongs consent.—
You, that make us unrighteous tribute pay,
See your own wealth as foully snatched away,
And, while permitted to despoil your brothers,
Submit, yourselves, to *be* despoiled by others.

We need not catalogue the various ways
In which now England on our country preys.
All know them well, while all must keep in view,
As still she wounds, she still despises too.
Crowning her insults with a vicious jest,
She sends, as guardian of our interest,
A feeble witling, whose high place to fill
Requires sound virtue, aided by nice skill
To know our state, our progress oversee,
Oppose each grief and urge prosperity.

See where the offspring of a world-famed sire
Would to a like celebrity aspire:
His seeming claim—the child must needs inherit
The parent's genius and each mental merit.
But higher animals engender mules,
And sons of clever men are often fools.—
The father's intellectual estate
Can scarce descend indeed: more elevate
The son's will be, or, else, degenerate.

(11) On any Irish grievance, not of a sectarian nature, none of our Journals write more strongly than those that are in the interest of the *Mission*.

Well doth our hero's character express
This truth, and by the sign of witlessness:
Ever prepared in Fame's pursuit to run,
Ambition calls and Folly drives him on.
The first crazed acts that signalized his name
Were in a foreign land, to Britain's shame.—
One party's enemy, the friend of none,
Mid frenzied mischief were his laurels won,
And him, whose faculties were tested thus,
Contempt and malice send to watch o'er us.

So hither in a luckless hour he flies,
And public judgment then at once defies.
'Gainst feeling proof, impervious to shame,
"*Two rows of pins he cares not*" for our blame.
Rich in that firmest kind of confidence
That holds no place in part with common sense,
He seems all bluster and unmeaning antic—
Stupidity by egotism made frantic.
Yet while to lofty trust the raver strides,
The clamorous bully to mute fear subsides;
For though at people he can snarl and yelp,
If they endure it, like the currish whelp,
He, cur-like too, if they for fight prepare,
Runs off and *slinks beneath his master's chair;*
And while to certain shelter thus he flies,
And all amends for insult still denies,
There's nothing left his foe but—to despise.

So brave is he, so wise and so refined,
Into whose hands are we, poor Celts, consigned!
And, in his famous attributes elate,
He issues forth to judge the nation's state,

His task performing with such intellect
And with such care as we must needs expect,—
Careful lest observation might impede
His froward fancy or his railway speed,
And just so cautious mid his foolish freaks
As to make sure to find not what he seeks.

So, while he headlong scours the country round
Where the loud cries of shivering want resound,
Against its obvious marks he shuts his eyes,
And its existence, thus disproved, denies.
His grudge against a town and envied bay
He well discloses with a kick and bray,
And hastes from Galway in a fume and flurry
To fool more foolish Orangemen in Derry.
The bright finale—he makes up his mind
That he perceived not what he did not find,—
That, looking not, he saw no suffering poor;
And so concludes his reasoning and his tour.

If now in Parliament he sets his face
'Gainst what he favored in another place;
If rightful pledges broken show in him
That promised good is but a fleeting whim—
Pledges to aid the amendment of bad laws—
Say not designing falseness is the cause.—
Declare him innocent, who wants a mind
With power for design of any kind.—
Without an aim when promises he makes,
He still has none when promises he breaks.—
See then nor vice nor virtue in those acts:
Witless he pledged and witless too retracts.

He differs from the wind-vane just in this:
That in his shuffles any *cause* we miss.
Each fault may vex, but let us still not view it
As plotted sin; for he's not equal to it.
Let him be tried where charity arraigns,
And freed of guilt, because absolved of brains.

God help the land where hating powers rule,
And sift contemptuous hatred through a fool!
If ours be not that land, still you and we
Unnumbered grievances in common see;
While you, to keep your brethren still in thrall,
Though oft complaining, yield assent to all.

We yet by a sad history are taught,
In all the evils you have ever wrought
Upon us Catholics in fiercest hate,
Even Catholics with you were federate.
How many, thus, have ever stood professed
Foes of their country's fame and interest!
How many, too, have only watched the hour
In which they might attain to place and power,
When for the principles they seemed to cherish,
And well proclaimed by loud rhetoric flourish,
The price were offered, and they might retreat
From honor to some governmental seat!
Yet by our country traitors are believed
The same as if she never was deceived.
Her long experience fails to make her see
The plain befooling ways of treachery:
For Ireland, famed for soundness in her faith,
In politics but feeble judgment hath.

But when, from time to time, she finds revealed,
Among her sons, each traitor long concealed,
Who loudest claimed, perhaps, to love her well,
While you, plain constant foes on principle,
In a low place your native land would keep,
The hapless land can scarce do more than weep.
What can she more when grievances oppress
Only by her own sons' unfaithfulness?
And hence the apathy with which she bears
Her wrongs, while not a look of hope she wears.
The same curst cause of hopelessness we see
From even her first page of history;
And thus, while hers should be a sprightly mien,
Yet so to grief she has accustomed been,
Her furrowed brows denote the long distress,
Though transient sparklings of her eyes confess
The native impulse of light-heartedness.
And, though her genius for the light and gay
Is eminent, yet sorrow's ancient sway
Has so engaged it, that it seems to rise
Ever the most inspired mid tears and cries.
This we observe, when, haply, we explore
Erin's traditions and poetic lore:—
This in her music may be well perceived—
Most felt by stricken souls that most have grieved,
And showing, in its grandest, brightest flow,
The fullest throbbings of her heart of woe;
Even as the glitter of the billow's crest,
Pulsed into radiance, proves the sea's unrest.
    Behold our Erin then personified,
Sitting in sorrow by some river's side;

When the moon lights the yellow-flowered meads,
And sadly rustle the dark quivering reeds;
When lilies, that upon the water sleep,
Bear up bright beauty from the sombre deep,
And the night-perfumes of low meadows lie
Where reed-wrens sing and shadowy plovers fly.
Or we may fancy that she rests upon
Some silent hill, dejected, weary, wan.—
Let us imagine the lone seat she seeks
Is among Binnabeola's desert peaks,[12]
When land and sea are now, perhaps, arrayed
In a rich garb of autumn's light and shade.
See her bent figure, that the old woes oppress,
On Bennacoir's high stony nakedness.
A faded shamrock-wreath her forehead wears:
In her cold hand a broken crown she bears:
A stringless harp one side unnoticed lies;
And at her feet a faithful wolf-hound dies.
With mourning aspect her sad soul imbues
The wide and wondrous scene that she now views.—
Around her rise the tempest-furrowed heights,
Where undisturbed the lonely eagle lights.
Streaked by the quartz, the deeply channelled sides
Of clustering mountains hold the torrents' tides,
That, from the cliffs, midst oak and holly leap,
And to Loch Ina's peaceful waters sweep.

　　High-rising from those waters' moory shore,
Maam Ean's bare indented ridges soar.
The plain of Moyrus sparkles in the sheen
Of countless lakes with dusky wastes between;

(12) Binnabeola.—" The Twelve Pins," Connemara.

Though tinted banks their waters oft enfold,
Set in the bloom of heath, like gems in gold.
On that far hill's dark side the jagged line
Of an impeded stream is seen to shine;
If we might fancy a forked lightning's gleam
Fixed on the storm-gloom, so appears that stream.
   Beyond those rolling ranges, far away
Yet seeming near, a sun-lit cone of grey,
O'er the brown tumult of the mountain-sea,
Shines, island-like, in single majesty:
A monument that nature's self supplies—
Fine-tapered and far stretching toward the skies,
And consecrated to our Christian fame
With its old honor of Saint PATRICK's name.
   Above those heights that shade the "Lake of
     deers"
Imperial Muilrea's towering form appears.
Supreme, a mighty space of heaven he fills;
Nor his the aspect of these nearer hills.
No rugged features does the observer see
In his calm, swelling, solemn majesty.
High from his base of porphyry he springs,
And holds the forms of ancient living things.
Strange shapes of many an extinct ocean race
He clasps, indeed, within his hard embrace;
And in his vastness wondrously arise
Old records of sea-life amid the skies.
   Now there the ocean sends his billowy host
On full a hundred miles of serrate coast.
Mid the white waves from north to south along
Bare rocks arise and fruitful islands throng.—

Clare Isle, once famous for her pirate queen,
Rising to guard that northern bay is seen.
The lower form of Bofin, in a vest
Of purple, streaks the waters to the west.
Southward fair Arran shows her long extent,
Renowned for sacred fane and monument.
Beyond the glistening "Bay of yellow sands,"
Whose breadth from many a sinuous cove expands,
Those islet-rocks, that vision scarce defines,
Hold Saint MacDara's and Saint Killian's shrines;
And isles unnamed and countless, far and near,
Skirt the long coast and in each bay appear;
While ocean, to the horizon's vapory shrouds,
Seems islanded with shadows of the clouds.

Dimly in distance and the southern glare,
More like a thickening of a point in air,
Than aught of earth, is seen the lofty shape
Of Brandon, who looks down on many a cape.
In the south-east the distant prospect fills
With the blue curves of Burren's round-topped
      hills.
Ascending platforms made by ancient tides,
Like stairs of giants, mark their circled sides.
O'er Galway's bay they stand, as if designed
To shield its harbors from the south-west wind:—
And I have seen, on many a summer's day,
When summer's peace on earth and ocean lay,
In the smooth deep their pictured heights assume
The semblance of fallen drapery of gloom;
And where the long low swell unruffled rolled
I marked the waving of the curtain's fold.

Beyond Benleva's side, remote and dim,
Dotting the eastern faint horizon's rim,
With the broad level girt on every side,
Knock Maa—"the mountain of the plain"—is spied.
Within his caverned breast, old legends tell,
A fairy tribe and *King Finvarra* dwell.
And often, when the low, full, midnight moon
Fronts the arched twilight of the north in June,—
While still the cuckoo signals his retreat,
And in the dew of hawthorns bathes his feet,
And all, save his night-loudened voice, is still,—
Then, suddenly, around the haunted hill,
A sound is heard, first like a gentle breeze
Through young soft leaves, or like the hum of
　　　bees:—
Then, rising to a roar as unsubdued
As winter's tempest through the naked wood,
It pours full onward far across the fair
Unclouded open of the fragrant air,
And in the uncertain distance is soon lost:—
So issues from Knock Maa the elfin host.

Now o'er the mountain tops that intervene,
Still in the utmost limits of the scene,
Nephin appears—his lofty pyramid
In masses of north-eastern clouds half hid :
While summits reared behind him to the west,
Some in the gauzes of grey vapor dressed,
And some appearing in unclouded blue,
Complete the outer circle of the view.
　　Such is the varied prospect that invites
To Binnabeola; mid whose lonely heights

We may thus fancy that our Erin mourns
For long lost hope that never still returns.
Replete with charms indeed, the land we boast—
Its hills, vales, rivers, lakes, its plains, its coast :
The fairest lines of loveliness it shows ;
And while with sweetest grace its beauty glows
In many a broad expanse of brightest green
It seldom frowns even in the mountain scene.
No threatening grandeur of an Etna there:
No icy terrors poised in Alpine air :
No torrents of wide desolating flow :
No sliding ruin of o'erwhelming snow ;
And though, at times, we may not vainly seek
For desolation of the rocky peak,
Or terror speckled in the cliff beneath
With the green holly and the purple heath,
Yet beauty crossed with no terrific trait
Our hilly landscapes oftenest display :—
Soft-swelling beauty their smooth curves express;
And dimpled beauty is their ruggedness.
    But why to those fair scenes for ever cling
The arms of poverty and suffering ?
Favoured by nature in a generous soil,
And in a hardy race inured to toil,
Our land in wealthy produce overflows,
Yet cannot part from famine's constant woes.[13]
What can this sad anomaly explain ?
The *Church Establishment* that you maintain !

(13) It is well known that, even during the famine years, Ireland
produced more food than would be sufficient for her wants if it had
been kept for her own use.

In this, already, I have shown the springs
' Of our great weakness and our sufferings.—
Where one strong section of an humbled race
Seek not themselves to reach a higher place,
But to keep down the rest is their sole view,
Content, if uppermost, to stay down too—
The land where this may be can never rise,
Though fine its features, and though mild its skies:
So Erin hapless, helpless, hopeless lies.

And is there yet no hope, that we shall see
At length an end of your hostility,
When virtue shall be vouchsafed from above
To chase the fiend that binds your patriot love?
Indeed with voice of triumph we are told
That now in Ulster, your well-loved stronghold,
An obvious miracle is taking place,
A sure *revival* of old gospel grace.
Happy, indeed, if this recoil from sin
Were truly, as you state it, genuine!
We then might hope to see your spirit freed
From those vile bonds that that blest love impede—
Love for your brethren of all doctrines, and
Love for the honor of our common land.
But in those famed *Revivals* you revere
No grounds as yet for such fair hopes appear;
And Papists well may doubt the fancied source
Of all this seemingly religious force,
And less with reverence than with surprise,
Regard those faintings and those maniac cries.
Surely to us the matter must seem droll,
That seeking grace, the flesh outvies the soul,

Swooning to righteousness, where, if you faint
And get up mad, you rise a remade saint !
Here we should say that the reformers still
Only revive their famous ancient skill, ·
Which shows to us how ill the Scripture chimes
With truth, as they would have it, in these times:—
So madness, as the Gospel writers tell,
Was *cured* by dispossessing fiends of hell ;
But here blest spirits with the curst change place,
And *giving* madness seems the act of grace.
Yet no true grace in this can Papists see—
Papists so quite unused to novelty ;
Yet if you say we wrongly judge indeed,
And those *Revivals* must from grace proceed,
Before our admiration can be caught,
Let us be shown what changes they have wrought :
Let us be shown the proofs that they afford
Of having drawn you nearer to the Lord.
Beneath their influence, so highly prized,
Have Ulster's Orangemen been Christianized ?
But how the zealots have to Christ been moved,
By the fresh blood of Lurgan be it proved ! [14]

(14) The shooting of a number of Papists, chiefly women and children, by the orangemen at Lurgan or Derrymacash on the "*glorious anniversary*," of Aghrim, 1860, shows how far the *Revivals* have effected the christianizing of that class. However, that at least the *name* of Christ is not repudiated by them may be gathered from the evidence on the magisterial investigation that followed. An example of the way in which the Blessed Name was used on the occasion is found in the testimony of a witness, who, after describing the beating of a girl by the orangemen, one of whom "had a hold of her by the hair of the head, and was kicking her, and had a stone in his other hand," said that he heard another, whom he named, " swearing by his ' *Holy J—; was there no man to give him a cap* (percussion

Then shines no hope in those "Revivals" strange
Of any great and truly moral change,
Which might at length the dire fanatics lead
To take in love and mercy to their creed,
And view us Papists as their brethren true—
Children of the same God and country too.

While in far Syria the martyr dies,
Or from the furious assassin flies—
While Christians sink beneath the unsparing sword
Of Turk or Druse or Bedouin or Kurd—
While slaughter shrieks across the land's whole
   breadth,
And Lebanon's old cedars wave o'er death,
Our Orange rivals of the Druse make known
Their zeal, and have a slaughter of their own.
Thus Orangeman and Druse seem well agreed
In the chief means by which they prove their
   creed;
But with this difference—the former brute
Beyond comparing is the more astute.
The one runs headlong, furious without sense,
Nor waits to calculate the consequence:

cap) *till he would shoot!*" (Reported in *the Freeman's Journal* of July
20, 1860.)

But in justice to the orangeman of this country we must say that
he stands not alone in his propensity to spill Catholic blood. His
relative, the Dutchman, seems not a little inclined that way, where
he can gratify his desires with impunity. In Mr. Oliphant's paper on
Japan, read before the British Association at Aberdeen in 1859, he tells
us, (I quote from the *Manchester Guardian* of September 24,) that the
siege of Simabarra "*forms a celebrated but melancholy episode in the
history of Christianity in Japan. 85,000 Roman Catholic Christians,
who had taken refuge within its waters, were bombarded by the Dutch
at the behest of the Japanese government, and utterly exterminated.*"

The other, not less eager, but more wise,
Would put his killing in a lawful guise.
The Orange *matador* essays to drag
His victim to assault, and waves his flag;
Then, mid exciting plaudits, he resents
The charge, and kills, as 'twere, in self-defence.
But, if his tenets still are best pursued
Where he gets drunk in revelry of blood,
Let not his ire for Druse-like carnage shriek;
But even Druse-like assassins let it seek.
His prowess he may justly thus direct,
And earn the praise of every Christian sect—
His slaughter no feigned gospel to extend,
But persecuted Christians to defend.
But no! that task of charity and grace
Is not assigned to a relentless race.
And though the hostile Orange volunteer
Before Rome's walls would willingly appear,
To save the Christian from pursuing swords
No help his pious sympathy affords;
And, indeed, England, whom he so esteems,
Less anti-Druse than anti-papal seems.
Not hers those standards on the Syrian shore,
Where she, when faithful, raised the cross of yore;
Where she, when Catholic, wrought deeds of fame,
And Moslems trembled at her Richard's name.
The flags of France they are, that brightly wave:
Of France, come not for conquest, but to save;
Come in her strength all Catholic and great,
To shield the Christian from the martyr's fate.[15]

(15) All true Christians must deplore the departure of the French
army from Syria before the establishment of more permanent

While thus the soldiers of the cross may claim,
In a good cause undoubted Christian fame,
Let Orangemen their brethren slay at home
And blood their bibles in their hate of Rome,
Thus the dread MISSION's destiny fulfil,
And be the deadly scourge of Christians still.

Yet this old passion of the Orange brood
Is now illegal, if still unsubdued;
And as the altered law their wrath impedes,
Few, in proportion, are their murderous deeds.
The *right* of murder, once the common boast
Of all your missionaries, is now lost;
So its effect your preacher seldom tries,
But proves his spirit by abuse and lies :—[16]

security for the Christian inhabitants. The premature withdrawal
of their best protectors is to be ascribed to the strict fulfilment of a
treaty, insisted on, as it is said, by the English government, contrary
to the wishes, as it is also reported, of even Russia, who would have
the stay of the French troops prolonged.

(16) As to their favorite weapons of abuse and slander, it is hard to
say by what Scripture our Anglican missionaries can justify their
use of them against the faith of others. Even among the Jews such
conduct was discountenanced. Josephus makes Moses say "let no
one blaspheme those Gods which other cities esteem such." (*Anti-
quities B. IV. s.* 10.) The same command occurs in the English
Bible as follows—"Thou shalt not revile the Gods, nor curse the
ruler of thy people." (*Exod.* xxii. 28.) By the interpretation of this
passage the word "*Gods*" is said to signify *magistrates*, but from
Josephus we may infer that the Jews took it in its literal sense, as
denoting the false Gods of the Heathen; and we must admit that the
Jewish principle of abstaining from any cause of offence to one's
neighbour on account of his religion was well worthy of the grand
tenet of Christianity, which would have peace and good will among
men. However, we need not go to Judaism for this excellent precept. It was not the habit of the apostles to deprecate the Pagan
deities in the spirit of insult. In the speech of Alexander to the
excited Ephesians he maintained that Paul and his disciples were

Thus where fanatic wrath in days of old
Would make the preacher slay, your preachers scold,

"*neither guilty of sacrilege nor blasphemy against their goddess*"
(Acts xix. 37.) But the command of this forbearance is more especially made known to us by St. Jude, who tells us that "*when
Michael the archangel, disputing with the devil, contended about the
body of Moses, he durst not bring against him the judgment of railing speech, but said: The Lord command thee.*" (St. Jude v. 9.) St.
Jude's denunciations of those, who, on the contrary, incline to the
abusive style of controversy and *blaspheme whatever things they
know not*, (v. 10, see also 2 Peter ii. 11, 12.) like the Catholic sacraments, may well be studied by our Anglican missionaries. And it
may be noticed that the "railing speech" of these preachers is not
directed even against Pagan deities, nor the devil himself, but against
Christians.

The following will give an idea of *Missionary* argumentation.—
The *Castlebar Telgeraph* of February 11, 1852, in an article on the
burning of effigies of the Blessed Virgin in London, asks—"*But
what shall we say of a man, claiming the office of a clergyman, who
the other day in Westport, exhibited in a gathering of people, what
he called a wafer, similar to that used in the Host in the Catholic
Church? This wafer he held up to the audience, and to show it
possessed neither life nor blood, he dissected it with his knife, and
next, in his holy zeal, rubbed it beneath his clerical boot in the dirt.*"

A reverend Anglican missionary is reported to have admitted on
his oath at the Castlebar Assizes, that he told the people their
religion was damnable and idolatrous; and, to justify himself, he
added that he swore it, and that the Queen swore it. To swear it as
a legal requirement was a matter for his own conscience, but thus
insultingly to proclaim it was quite another thing, and precisely
characteristic of the "missionaries to Roman Catholics."

A minister of the *Establishment*, the Rev. Mr. Townsend, who was
examined on the trial of *Lavelle v. Bole* in Galway, at the Summer
Assizes, 1860, admitted (according to the report in the *Freeman's
Journal*) that he told the plaintiff, the Rev. Father Lavelle, of Partry,
that he was "*a minister of Antichrist*," and swore that he *still*
believed him to be a minister of Antichrist. Contrast this with the
evidence of the reverend plaintiff, and the *animus* of each party—
the "*saints*" of THE MISSION, and their hated opponents—may be
correctly estimated.—Father Lavelle, in his cross-examination by
Mr. Fitzgibbon, gave his opinion of the *missionary schools* as follows:
"*I will not say the doctrines taught in these schools are damnable;*

And show how certainly the Spirit ran,
To *wretched swine*, from the *outrageous man*.[17]
Such are your pleaders, who for ever scream,
Belying men, and God Himself blaspheme,
To swear their doctrine into our esteem—
Who strangely thus among our poor contest
The place of trust and reverence with *the Priest*,
And tell them as an enemy to view
The only real friend they ever knew—
In every grief their refuge and defence,
In sin, oppression, want and pestilence.

But where the "*saints*" would thus persuade to
hate,
They only show more cause to venerate.
The priest's right influence then mocks their spite,
Vainly displayed by what they speak or write, .
Or by the Scripture-*pistol* cocked upon
Some text of Mark or Matthew, Luke or John.[18]

*I will say they are false; my belief is they are not anti-Christian,
but they are not all in their entirety, the doctrines of Christ.*"
Father Lavelle described how he was addressed by a *saintly* contro-
versialist who "commenced to abuse the Catholic church, its ministers, its practices and its teachings. He then told me I was the
devil, and put out his tongue at me."—Enough of *missionary*
argumentation!

(17) Luke viii. 33.

(18) The pistol which the Rev. Mr. Goodison, evangelical minister,
produced in his dispute with the Rev. Father Lavelle, P.P. of Partry,
will hardly, serve to alienate from him the affections of his flock. I
extract the following from a London paper of high repute, the
Examiner, which contained an article on the first legal investigation
regarding this theological feat. "However, here we have the Rev.
Mr. Goodison admitting that he broke out upon the priest, who had
given him no provocation, but had accosted him in the most civil
manner, with the above impertinent and offensive questions. As we
must suppose that they were put by the roving missionary in the

Yet if they fail to charm us by abuse,
Or clamorous threat, both still have real use :
These are the means by which they keep alive
The zeal of those who hope their preachings thrive—
The noisy *advertising* of the trade :
And by the noise supporting dupes are made,
Whose ready purses piously repay
The arts of every gospel *Holloway.*
So, in the end, though much those arts debase,
They keep the preachers in their saintly place—
The ballast of the ship that bears the knaves,
Tending to sink it, yet from sinking saves.
But they, who dream not still that knave or " saint "
Will gain the wealthy or intelligent,
And whose most daring hope is to allure
To England's doctrine our unlearned poor,

exercise of his functions under the Society which employs him, it is
easy to understand why they feel it necessary to provide their
agents with pistols. Although the Irish are not the fire-eating people they formerly were, it is obvious that any man who makes it his
business to ride about the country, addressing irritating observations on the most exciting of subjects to every member he meets of
the persuasion or order to which they must be most disagreeable,
ought in common prudence to be armed against the chance of meeting with dangerous tempers. We may therefore judge of the pro-
priety of the missionary's proceedings by his previous martial pre-
parations. His revolver explains his religion ; his pistol exhibits in
the strongest possible light the decency of his catechism. This is
perfectly independent of the questions which are reserved for trial.
We should like to see the Church Missionary Society itself brought
to justice for sending such as Mr. Goodison abroad through a
country like Ireland, where they are under the necessity of going
armed in apprehension of assaults, provoked, if not justified, by
their own misbehaviour. The men of whom it is said that their
footsteps were ' beautiful on the mountains,' were not missionaries
of the stamp that roam on the mountains of Mayo."

Behold the best of England's Church at home
Ever departing for the fold of Rome.
Their hate of her, thus stung to rabidness,
Storms in the pulpit, rages in the press.
But all the shades their hate around her throws
Tend but her present greatness to disclose ;
As when upon the moon earth's shadows dull
Would quench her light, they prove her at the full.[19]

(19) The following extract from the *London Telegraph* relating to the conversions in a *single district* in London, will serve to show the extent and character of Catholic progress in England :—

" St. Paul's, Knightsbridge, seems destined to maintain its reputation as furnishing more examples of secession from the Church of England than any other metropolitan district. A correspondent informs us that, in addition to former converts, the Rev. Messrs. Fothergill and Wormal, curates of that parish, have just seceded from the Established Church—the one from St. Paul's, the other from St. Barnabas—and have since been received into the Church of Rome. Since the erection of the two churches mentioned, it is asserted, on good authority, that eight curates, between thirty and forty peers, members of parliament, &c., together with a large number of ladies and gentlemen residing in the district, have been added to the list of converts."

The *Morning Advertiser* gives a list of nearly 130 members of the University of Oxford, chiefly clergymen with high collegiate honors, who had seceded to the Church of Rome, up to February, 1859.

The *National Protestant Society* finds that Catholicity is making immense strides in England. According to a report read before it by Mr. Harper, showing the progress of Roman Catholicism during the last twenty years, " the number of priests has been doubled ; the chapels in 1840 were 522, and they were now 950 ; the monasteries had increased from 8 to 87, and the nunneries from 20 to 128, not including the abodes of Tractarian sisterhoods, under the sanction of some of the bishops of England."

The secretary informed the startled and astonished audience that a "list of clergymen numbering one hundred and fifty-one, of whom twenty-one belonged to the diocese of London, who had signed a *document recognizing Transubstantiation and the Mass*, had been obtained by the conference: and a resolution had been passed, praying the bishops who were over these clergymen to take the proper steps concerning them."

There is no doubt of the rapid spread of Catholicity among the educated classes in England, nor can its increase there be counterbalanced by the "*exterminating*" *gospel* in the West. It is worthy of observation that, in England, *the converts to Catholicity are principally anglican clergymen and others who are best qualified to judge between the Churches.* The number of those who sacrifice their worldly prospects for the ancient Faith, and *without any missionary endeavors* on the part of the Catholics, is indeed quite remarkable. On the other hand, the few unfortunate priests, who, *after being suspended and disgraced* in their own Church, are received with open arms by the Anglicans, are not, in any way, worthy of notice; and what shall we say of the unnamed, unproved, and, indeed, quite mythical conversions that are claimed by the Anglican missionaries as the result of the expenditure of those sums of £30,000 or £40,000 that so inspire their saintly ardor among the Celts? (See report of missionary meeting in the *Irish Times*, April 9th, 1861.)

Apropos of statements made at missionary meetings it may be observed that the favorite plan is to boast of *deeds performed* when alluding to the money that was expended, trying to satisfy the donors by assuring them of its good effects: but when asking for *more* money the tone is different, and here it would seem that the interests of the MISSION demand a less complete departure from truth. It is no longer the good that *was* done, but the good that *might* be done if people would only continue their old liberality. In an advertisement published in the *Times* of June 5, 1861, the missionary committee deplores a falling off in the subscriptions to the amount of £2000 a year, which will necessitate a corresponding restriction of the field of operations; and this is the more to be lamented as in the places about to be vacated "the most favorable symptoms are apparent, showing that great progress has been made in enlightening the minds of Roman Catholics, and *preparing* for an effectual conversion of many to a spiritual life." Here the good is all *in prospectu;* and who with missionary sympathies can keep his purse strings tightened with such a view before him? Yet the committee seems not very sanguine about replacing the lost £2000. and with a pathetically expressed resignation "feel it to be their duty humbly to submit to the will of God." A gleam of hope, however, shines in the conclusion of the address, where it is remarked that "perhaps it may be God's will to avert some, if not all, the distressing results of the present necessity, by suggesting liberal and ready help as the only means of preventing this serious check to the progress of the great cause."

ANGLICANIA.

—

PART II.

s

PART II.

All reasonable men might well inquire
Whence can arise the MISSION'S furious fire:
For what true purpose the sectarian wrath
Against Rome's doctrine—Ireland's ancient faith.
Is not the Scripture's free interpretation
To each one granted by the Reformation?
And how then, Anglicans, can you object
To *any* creed a Christian may select?
Free judgment you proclaim; and why insist,
That tenets Anglican must not be missed?
Each is his own interpreter to be,
Yet, strange, with you must dare not disagree!
   Yet blaming here means not that we defend
Free judgment for the use that *you* commend,
Which, first we'll say, when you would proselyte
In favor of it, seems a puzzle quite:
For by *interpretation* of *your own*
The claim of free interpreting is shown;
But now, if *you* expound for *us*, are we
Truly as self-interpreters left free?
Real free judgment must be left at rest:
Free judgment to "free judgment" can't be pressed;
And if to your persuading we should bend,
That same free judgment that you taught would end:
So, therefore, by strange consequence, your thesis,
When just demonstrated, should fall to pieces;
And their own doctrines they, indeed, befool,
Who only *by its breaking prove their rule.*

To *choose* our church do *we* free judgment use,
But not its bonds of doctrine then to loose.
Contented with the freedom to select
Our guide, we follow as he may direct:
But *your* free judgment is, forsooth, so bright,
That even the guide himself it would set right.
No wonder, if from this self-trust proceeds
A Babel-scandal of unnumbered creeds;
For those who on free judgment so insist
Are like men wandering scattered through a mist:
While all the others in thick fog appear,
Each thinks the space around himself is clear,
Yet, notwithstanding, strays he knows not where.[20]

(20) The inevitable diversity that characterizes the opinions of
religious reformers, and which gave at least sixteen well defined
sects to the Manicheans, at least eighteen, according to Gibbon
(Decline and Fall, c. xxi.) to the Arians, and a number not to be
counted to the Protestants, became apparent among the last named
at the earliest stages of their history. We may instance their
variety of doctrine relating to the Real Presence. Huss admitted
transubstantiation, but differed from the Catholics about communion
in two kinds: Luther denied it, but pronounced for consubstantiation
Zuinglius denied both: Calvin's doctrine is contradictory and puz-
zling. In his Treatise on the Lord's Supper, he proves that Luther
and Zuinglius misunderstood each other, *and are both wrong.* He
said that he did not dispute about the presence and substantial eating, but the *manner* of both. He said, in his *Institutions,* that as the
Holy Ghost was under the form of a dove, so the body of Jesus
Christ is under the form of bread; he said that the Eucharist was an
extract of the flesh of Jesus Christ in the condition in which it is in
Heaven. He gave various other expositions of the doctrine with
which he appeared never able to satisfy himself, and deplored in his
letter to Melancthon the divisions among reformers, saying that *it
was ridiculous beyond imagination, that, after having separated themselves from the whole world, they could so little agree among themselves
since the commencement of their reform.* (See Bossuet's Variations.)
Similar differences existed between the reformers in other matters
of faith, in original sin, baptism, predestination, &c. and they con-

On our own wit, then, *we* do not depend
Our faith against false tenets to defend.
Supposing that the *church* might go astray,
How could *we, singly*, hope to find the way?
Would God from the communion take his creed,
And this to individuals concede?
Or if God wanted power to maintain
Would not man's efforts to restore be vain?
We'd cease to be, if here we thought like you,
Not only catholics, but christians too.

Yet on some points true doctrine might be found,
Though free interpretation should expound.
Faith and free judgment sometimes so concur,
That we might follow this and still not err.

tinually altered their own opinions, as we find in the various confes-
sions of faith made by them at different times. Robertson says
(Chas. V. B. V.) that Melancthon, who drew the confession of
Augsburg, "*softened some articles, made concessions with regard to
others and put the least exceptional sense on them all.*" Melancthon
himself, writing to Luther, admitted that he was obliged *often to
change them and accommodate them to the occasion. Every day he
changed and re-changed, and would have changed more if he had been
permitted by his companions.* (Bossuet: *Histoire des variations des
Eglises Protestantes*, l. iii, n. 63.) The Augsburg Confession, thus
prepared, and the great foundation of Protestantism, appears in four
different forms. (Bossuet, var. l. iii. n. 5.) The Saxon confession,
also written by Melancthon, differs from them; and the confession
of Smalcalde, to which he subscribed, differs from all the others (Id.
l. viii. n. 18, 19.) With what little *confidence* Protestantism was
worked out by its apostles! And Protestants reject the books of
the Machabees chiefly from an expression of the writer, suggesting
a want of confidence in himself! No wonder that the divisions and
subdivisions of the original sects, the fungi-growths from the
various unsound branches, are innumerable.

*I may here remark that in Bossuet's book, on which I draw largely,
will be found references to the works of the Reformers,* WHO, THEM-
SELVES, ARE HIS CONSTANT AUTHORITIES *for his statements respecting
them.*

In certain paths it well might guide us long,
While it, again, makes heretics go wrong.
Oft, acting like a trusty satellite,
It shines, reflecting Faith, and brings us right;
But then, at times, though long the light it kept,
Faith's broadest day 'tis sure to intercept.

As men's free judgment in religion moves,
Their self-esteem declares each step improves;
And who could mark the limits of its run
With the faith's reformation once begun?
If the old Church led men astray from Heaven
For fifteen centuries, or, say, eleven,[21]

(21) Whatever Protestants may allege in disproof of our Catholic doctrine relative to the Papal supremacy, they can't deny that it was certainly admitted at the Council of Chalcedon A. D. 451; where the legates of Leo, one of them an ordinary priest, took precedence of the bishops there assembled. The supremacy was plainly declared in the 4th act of the council, which stated that the rule of faith it followed was the same as that which was established at previous councils, and "*followed by Saint Leo, Apostolic man, and Pope of the universal church.*" Strange that Reformers should dissent from the council in this, and agree to its other decisions. Gibbon, alluding to this council, remarks that Europe during ten centuries received her religious opinions from the Vatican, and "*the same doctrine*"—that of the Incarnation—"*was admitted without dispute into the creed of the Reformers who disclaimed the supremacy of the Roman Pontiff.*" (Decline and Fall, c. xlvii.) This was near a century and a half before the mission of St. Augustin, from whom England received her Christianity; and that the same supremacy was acknowledged in his time, we may learn from St. Gregory the Great, who sent him there. The following passage from a letter of St. Gregory's to the Bishop of Syracuse will show that the great church of Constantinople was subject to the Apostolic seat of Rome—"*Nam de Constantinopolita ecclesia quod dicunt, quis eam dubitet Sedi Apostolicæ esse subjectam? Quod et piissimus dominus Imperator, et frater noster Eusebius ejusdem civitatis episcopus assidue profitentur.*" (Lib. 7, Indict. 2, Epist. 64.) And again, (E. 65) alluding to a bishop who lay under some accusation, he says—"*Nam quòd se dicit Sedi Apostolicæ subjici, si qua*

Is it not possible yourselves, for three,
May have gone wrong, if even in less degree?
And even supposing truth was surely gained,
Still the whole truth may not be yet obtained.
Then how to Mormon or "Essayist" show,
That reformation should not farther go
Than your *Establishment*, where faith must find
The last improvement that the Lord designed?
Changes *required*, would show it his intent,
As in material development,
That creeds improved should have successive birth,
Like geologic eras of the earth;

culpa in episcopis invenitur, nescio quis ei episcopus subjectus non sit. Cum vero culpa non exigit, omnes secundum rationem humilitatis æquales sunt." I even find in Michaelis's proofs of the authenticity of the New Testament, *appended to the* ANGLICAN BIBLE, that the heretic, Marcion, early in the 2nd. century, travelled from Sinope to Rome, "*in order to obtain a repeal of the excommunication which had been denounced against him by his native church.*" This looked very like Rome's supremacy, and at a sufficiently early age too. But the objections of the Anglicans, seemed not, really, to be against *a* head, but *the* head of the church; for, in emancipating themselves from the Pope, they established a papacy of their own much more despotic than his: for instance, we read in *Burnet's History of the Reformation*, that Henry held the place of Pope in England; and Edward the Sixth's ecclesiastical jurisdiction may be understood from a letter to the Archbishop of York, wherein he says that, *being speedily to order a visitation over his whole kingdom, therefore neither the archbishop nor any other should exercise any jurisdiction while it lasted.* (Bohn's 8vo. edition, 1857, p. 808.) No wonder that such *a Pope* could *excommunicate*, and he ordered his injunctions relating to the visitation to be observed *under the pains of excommunication, sequestration, or deprivation, as the ordinaries should answer it to the King, the Justices of the Peace* being required to *assist them.* (Ibid, p. 809.) Among the injunctions it may be observed were directions for saying HIGH MASS, and praying "*for souls departed this life, that on the last day we may rest with them both body and soul.*" (Ibid.)

And that Reformers truly thought it so,
Their changes and improvements seem to show.
No matter what new doctrinal decree ;
You cannot blame it with consistency.
There's nothing strange where other men reduce
Your points of faith, as you think ours profuse.
On your own principle it seems not odd,
If still in this reduction men will plod,
And even at length exclaim "no Christ!"—"no
    God !"—
So far withdrawing from the ancient grief
Of "error," that they reach full unbelief.
Nor from Religion is it hard to stray,
When men explore by simple reason's ray,
Whose power then is even to make less bright,
Like the dark force of photographic light ;
And Faith, ballooning toward improvement's sun,
Not into heat but deadly cold must run.[22]

(22) The characteristic genius of Reformers, displayed in the
faculty of *reducing* and *simplifying* points of faith, is now well illustrated in England, where the doctrines of the famous "*Essays and
Reviews*," propounded by gentlemen high in the Established Church,
are taking such deep root among the clergy. Most prominent too
in the march of Gospel improvement is the Creed of *Mormonism*,
whose missions are remarkably successful among the evangelicals of
England and Wales. The Mormons, like other Reformers, *found their
faith on Scripture*, and particularly on *the 5th verse of the 1st chapter
of St. James*. By his private interpretation of that text, Smith, who
was at first only the tool of Rigdon, thought himself justified in
seeking for further Revelation ; and hence the finding of the Book
of Mormon buried in the hill of Cumorah with the *Urim and
Thummim* of the Jews, which miraculously enabled him to translate
the discovered Scripture. Who can limit the wonders of the Reformation? I don't know how nearly the doctrines of the *Agapemone* in
England may be related to Mormonism. For an excellent account
of the latter, see the *Illustrirte Zeitung*, March, April, May, 1852.

Yet if decided limits you would draw
To mortal tampering with Heavenly law,
And show, when from the Papal Church you
    part,
Your stop's as arbitrary as your start;—
If thus you would conclusively reject
Improvement of your Church of England sect;
Which, we all know, has certainly agreed
To hold at least an *Athanasian creed*—
See, plainly manifest, the wondrous blot:
You are free interpreters—and you are not:
Claiming free judgment you would leave Rome's
    track,
And by denying it keep others back.

You may declare your pious labor goes
Not to improve, but merely recompose.
But, if improvement has not been your aim,
Still reformation seems no wiser claim—
To Christianity an equal shame:
For equal falseness would the Faith confess
By imperfection or unstableness.

So Catholics, who on Christ's church rely,
Reform or progress in the Faith deny.—
The Church, indeed, by acts of various dates,
Confirms the Old, but nothing new creates:
Old points of faith, at every time *believed*,
From time to time are *formally received;*
Nor inference of progress can we draw
Where only ancient customs are made law.

We never feared that Heaven-sprung rules
    might show
No truer force than those of earth below,

Where oft the wise, no doubt, may miss the way
Which fools will find, who only go astray.
But different the rules by Heaven supplied,
And, sure that these can never fail to guide,
We *reformation* of the Church arraign,
In every view, as impious and vain;
While, equally, *improvement*, we must see,
In doctrine Heaven-revealed is not to be.—[23]

(23) The infallibility of the Church, as well as the Papal supremacy, was clearly declared in the Council of Chalcedon, in the 5th
act of which it is stated that "*we renew the infallible faith of our
fathers assembled at Nice, Ephesus and Constantinople under Celestine
and Cyril,*" and that "*the predication of the faith is immutable from
the beginning.*" Yet Protestants now deny the infallibility of the
Church, which was as perfectly defined by the council as the doctrine
of the Incarnation, which they receive. But this strange eclecticism
did not always prevail; as they often insisted on the infallibility of
the church when it suited their purpose; and it is remarkable that,
in arguing against each other, their sects were generally obliged to
assume Catholic doctrines and defend themselves on Catholic grounds.
For instance, Melancthon, deploring the dissensions of the Reformers, writes to Camerarius that "*If Jesus Christ had not promised
to be with us to the consummation of time I should fear that Religion
would be altogether destroyed by those dissensions.*" On the Calvinistic
side, the Synod of Delpht (A. D. 1618) declared the same Catholic
doctrine, proved by the same text, in answer to the Remonstrants,
and said that "*when Pastors assembled from various countries to
decide, according to the word of God, that which is proper to be taught
in the Churches, one must be persuaded with a firm confidence that
Jesus Christ is with them according to his promise.*" (Bossuet, Var. l.
xiv, n. 75.) Luther asserts his infallibility and denies Free will as
follows :—"*Free will is a vain title—God causes evil in us as well as
good—the great perfection of faith is to believe that God is just,
although he makes us necessarily incur damnation by his will.*" "*God
pleases you when he crowns the unworthy ; he ought not to displease
you when he damns the innocent.*" He concludes with his infallibility,
saying that "*he does not say these things as examining them, but determining ; that he means not to submit them to the judgment of any one,
but counsels every one to yield his belief to them.*" (Bossuet, Var. l. ii.
n. 17.)

We cannot say the Christian faith diverged
From Moses' Law, but this in that was merged,
Where change or progress, as our Lord assures,
Is not to be as long as time endures.

You have not called Reformers, Saints inspired :
Then was it by mere genius they were fired ?—
While man, indeed, progresses where the stores
Of Nature are revealed when he explores,
'Tis plain, of course, that genius, rightly free,
Assists his progress by its liberty,—
Oft rightly scorning old pedantic rules—
Improvement's bane—that, in life's various schools,
A mirror hold, which scarcely shows us more
Than what's behind, and hides the view before.
But in Faith's tenets genius leads astray
And must give place to inspiration's sway.
Made as we are, we must on each rely,
While one does not the other's place supply ;
And genius, ample as its range may be,
Yet finds its bounds within mortality.

Genius, inconstant, shows at various times,
Appears in various men and various climes.
So it is seen when blessings it confers
In its true sphere, or in religion errs.
Thus periodic heresies are made,
And the unstable, by the million, swayed.
Mohammed by plain genius spread his creed,
And thus do other frauds in faith succeed.
Man's genius is a heavenly *gift ;* though all
Find it, indeed, not ready at their call ;
But inspiration, when vouchsafed by God,
Still remained His, and never was bestowed,

That, like the human attribute, our hearts
It might illume by casual fits and starts.
Its light, by an eternal source assured,
Once made to shine, is not to be obscured.
If ever it to darkness could give place,
God would be a defaulter in that case,
Then how depend on a new act of grace?

And if the Faith *could* taint within the Church,
Why with such confidence the Bible search?
You plainly state, the Bible is made out
Of writings which the Church did never doubt.
If this be true, (though Papists may protest)
The Church was ever of the Book possest;
Now, *with* the Bible, if the Church can swerve
From truth, to what, then, does the Bible serve?
In the Church erring, we can only see,
The Book to Faith gives no security.
And at this so enlightened present day,
What signs of sureness does the Book display?
Upon its sureness would your sects subsist;
But if 'tis sure, your sects ought not exist.

And yet 'tis sure, but not as *you* maintain:
Sure but to those to whom one sense is plain:
The sense to each not at the moment shown,
But, like the book itself, transmitted down.
The sense, thus by TRADITION testified,
Shows where Christ's promises were most applied:
Less to the Book by rude adventures tossed,
In which we know that many parts were lost.[24]

(24) There are various references in the New Testament to Scriptures which are no longer extant. I may mention the Epistle of
Paul to the Laodiceans, which he alludes to in his Epistle to the

And, prejudice aside, just let us think
What, after all, are paper, pens and ink:—[25]
Mere substances that humanly record,
And perishable even with God's word.
It is the spirit, rather than the page,
That is secure from man's or devils' rage.
The Word's protection, which concerns the soul,
Has been left free from physical control:
No graven stone to be effaced or broken,
Or book more frail received Christ's doctrine, spoken
For safe transmission and decreed to rest
Indelibly upon the *heart* impressed.[26]
Though all the book were lost or quite obscure,
Safe in Tradition Faith would still endure.[27]

Colossians, chap. iv, v. 16. The meaning of that verse, which has been made the subject of dispute, is clearly shown by the Right Rev. Dr. MacEvilly, Bishop of Galway, in his Exposition of the Epistles; a work distinguished for rare ability and research, and one that ought to be in the hands of every Catholic who reads our language. An allusion to another lost epistle will be found in 1 Cor. v. 9.

(25) 2 Cor. iii. 3. 3 St. John, 12.

(26) Jer. xxxi. 33. Heb. viii. 10.

(27) St. Irenæus, who was only third in descent from the Apostles, exclaims "what if the Apostles had not even left us the Scriptures; should we not, in this case have been bound to follow the order of that TRADITION which they have deposited in the hands of those to whose care they have confided the government of the churches? There are many barbarous nations that have received the faith in Jesus Christ, and that have followed this order, preserving without letters or ink the truths of salvation written in their hearts by the Holy Ghost; observing carefully the ancient TRADITION." St. Cyril, whose writings of the middle of the fourth century are admitted genuine by the Anglican writers Cave, Milles, &c. cautions us against receiving any book as divine except by the authority of the Church and Tradition (Cat. 4, n. 23, 35, 36.) St. Gregory of Nyssa, writing in the same century, says that Tradition from the Apostles is enough to condemn heretics (Or. 3. Contra Eunom. p. 123.) St. John

The Book's deficiency you must admit,
Yet seem to think your faith no worse for it;
And, being of the complete book deprived,
Whence is your doctrine, if complete, derived?
Of either of two sources there is need
To furnish the completion of the creed:—
Tradition of the faith of men inspired,
Or, else, new revelation is required;
But this you dare not say exists for choice,
And you reject the other's sacred voice.

And if no help to extant Holy Writ
You grant; so must your creed be incomplete.
Yet this you see not, and pretend to trace
A perfect plan from an imperfect base.
So to the Bible you require no gloss,
In spite of all obscurity or loss;
And by it only, scorning every aid,
You say a perfect Christian must be made.
While its sufficiency you thus maintain,
And rest on private judgment to explain,
Let us suppose a case, and try to test
The real soundness of this doctrine blest.—

Suppose, then, that you laid the book before
A creedless man; and that you did no more.

Chrysostom of the same period, whose prayer, adopted by the
Anglican church, makes him a good Protestant authority, says—
"It is clear that they (the apostles) did not deliver all things by their
epistles, but communicated also many things without writing, and
these likewise deserve our assent or faith. It is a tradition: make
no further inquiry." (Hom. 4. in 2 Thess. p. 532.) These sacred
writers flourished within the period that the church of Rome was a
true and a pure church as admitted by Protestants; and the genuineness of their works cannot be more fairly disputed than that of the
Scriptures which came down to us through the same hands.

Of explanation not a single word
You gave to show the truths within it stored:
He never saw the book until that hour,
Nor heard of the Divine Inspiring Power:—
We ask your self-reliant common sense,
What in that case would be the consequence:—
Would he, unaided, in the volume see
The various truths of Christianity?—
Would he each mystery of Faith receive,—
In the Man-God and Triune God believe,—
See plainly how each prophecy applied
To the Redeeming Deity who died,—
How the Old Law's severities were true,
Yet typified the mercies of the New,—
In short, would he become a Christian man,
Or, more precisely, a true Anglican,—
Take up his pen and give us, line for line,
The Articles you number thirty-nine?
I think you will not dare affirm he would:
Then how must your faith's rule be under-
        stood?—
A Rule containing all by Faith required,
And plainly teaching too, because inspired;
Conferring faith; and, made in faith so strong,
The self-interpreter cannot go wrong.
But see you not, this rule is vainly sought?
The Bible, to be useful, *must be taught.*
Before we read the Book, both you and we
Are told, as children, what we there must see.
Thus teaching is by all essential made,
Nor is it to our reasoning years delayed.

What then can your sound judgment have achieved,
When previous to its period you believed,
And faith was not *discovered*, but *received*?

Not in the Book, then, is our faith discerned
Unless, before we read, our faith is learned;
Plainly at fault without extrinsic aid,
Its insufficiency is thus betrayed;
And, surely, even the lamp of Holy Writ,
Before its light is given, must be lit.

And what unlettered myriads, to the end,
Must for their faith on others quite depend—
While no direct acquaintance do they gain
With even the *words* the Bible may contain!
And can they still be certain of its sense,
Who can't be certain of its mere contents?
Yet if, in spite of all objections clear,
In a quaint principle you persevere—
If still the BIBLE is among you shown,
As the SOLE RULE, by which THE FAITH is
          known—
If from the writing each must judge his creed,
God help your blind, and all who cannot read!
God help who can! for those remain unsure
Whether the book they *get* to read be *pure*:
If truly pure they still the book might call;
The whole's not there, and so—God help you all!

Would not, indeed, the reader I described
Have any thing but Christian faith imbibed?[28]

(28) It is no argument against the case I have put, to say that such
a one is not *likely* to occur. The *possibility* of its occurring justifies
it. A less extreme case, but one that is equally applicable to my
purpose, is at this moment supplied by the *Taepings* of China.
A missionary narrative, noticed in the "*Morning Chronicle*" of

Would not the Book to his unlearned glance
Seem but a doubtful history or romance,
Of contradictions numbering not a few,
In precept and historic record too?—
Here David has seven brothers,[29]—there but six: [30]
To which account shall we our faith affix?
Here must no staff be in the preacher's hand,—[31]
There he must carry one by clear command: [32]
Where plain discordances like these are found,
Whose judgment unassisted can expound?

    The truth is this—the Book, without a guide,
Has no man's reason ever satisfied.
There inspiration doubtlessly is found;
Yet verbal errors may, indeed, abound;
How know, then, the defective from the sound?
And scruple not about such faults to yield,
Or you may lose to sceptics the entire field.
And while, besides, the Scriptures that are missed
Are those, perhaps, that most would faith assist,
Unsure must be the doctrine that is gained
All from the Book alone and unexplained;
Nor thus seem strange your countless shades of
    schism
From pseudo-Popery to Rationalism,

April 6, 1861, informs us that their chief men are *well versed in the Scriptures* and are at least *anxious* to be Christians, declaring that "Christianity is the only true religion, and that the Bible is the word of God." Yet they are averse to instruction, and by their own free judgment have composed a belief that is far removed, indeed from Christian Doctrine.

(29) I. Kings, xvi.   (30) I. Chron. ii.

(31) Mat. x. 10.   (32) Mark vi. 8.

4

Which, slow-absorbed, even now, without a shock,
With freezing force dissevers your faith's rock.
And against this free judgment's dire excess
Your church authority is powerless—
Authority that you must still comprise
Within your wondrous faith which ratifies
Points that it simultaneously denies.—
For now your creed to judgment free impels;
Then ties it down with church-made articles:
As we make windows to let in the light,
Then blinds and curtains add—for fear they might.

So fails the Book; for when *in it alone*
We seek for Faith, no one sure Faith is shown.
And while it really supports the true,
Heretic faith is based upon it too;
Thus in the Church directing *we* confide,
Nor among many paths refuse the guide.

The Church, unshaken in each Bible brawl,
Is firm, indeed, because traditional.
Therefore, in judging, it defines the laws:
The Book is but a witness in the cause;—
Or we might say, Christ built the church for man,
And did not merely leave a written plan.

Christ therefore spoke, and wrote not; and we
    note
The Apostles, like Him, preached: they also wrote;
But then from prison, or a distant place,
To those *already* blest with Gospel grace,
Who did the saving truth well understand—[33]
Some for their faith even famed in every land.[34]

(33) I. John ii, 21. This fact is made evident in *all* the epistles.
(34) Rom. i, 8.

What then did perfect faith to them transmit,
Who were true christians ere the Apostles writ?—
The oral testimony that they heard,
And which, of course, to writing was preferred.
From spoken words was faith's true spirit caught:
Paul, writing, rather counselled friends than taught.
What John has written by precise command
Is just the part we least can understand.
When the Colossian people Paul addressed
He called them "Saints" and "Faithful," like the
    rest.[35]
He never preached to them, nor did he write [36]
Until they first received the Gospel's light;
Which it pleased God should not directly pass
From Paul, but through an envoy, Epaphras.[37]
He brought no letter; and the people heard
Not less true predication when transferred—
From God to Paul; to Epaphras from him.
What space or time makes God's tradition dim?
If what Paul told him Epaphras could tell;
Could those the latter taught not teach as well?
And how can miserable mortals dare
To fix the limits of Almighty care?
Or say that, after some unsettled space
Of time, Tradition must fall off from grace?
We see, indeed, destruction overtook,
In part, the mortal writing of the Book.
Books disappear; but, while man's race endures,
His spirit-book, Tradition, God secures.
'Twas placed within the archives of the soul,
And only copied on the parchment roll;

(35) Col. i, 2.   (36) Col. ii, 1.   (37) Col. i. 7.

Nor fully yet: the whole was never penned;
And parts, that were, not to our days descend.
The words, that in the copy have remained,
Were well compared and judged before retained:
Judged by the Church, who did their truth confess:
So thus "the Greater rightly judged the Less."
And now, while incomplete the copy shows,
And so obscure to the extent it goes,
That, as the Apostle warns us well indeed,
It brings destruction where the unlearned read, [38]
The traditive original contains
All that the *Writing* wants, and all explains. [39]

  'Tis vain to say, the faithless Pharisees
With *their* traditions did the Lord displease.
Why did He so condemn them? Hear the cause!—
They were quite adverse to the sacred laws.
Were *they* the Church—that hypocritic sect—
That God should their traditions so protect?
Had *they* the promise, that the Holy Ghost
Would not permit God's teaching to be lost?
Christ told them, *search the Scriptures,* and decide
If He not there was plainly testified.
His own, unwritten then, were not implied. [40]
Nor were they written, some of them, for long
After He died:—was Faith, meanwhile, all wrong?

---

(38) II. Peter iii, 16.

(39) Among the Scripture texts in favor of Tradition I may point out II. Thes. ii, 14. (in the Anglican Testament verse 15.) II. Thes. iii, 6. II. Tim. ii, 2. The testimony of the Fathers concerning it is very clear, and is sufficiently shown by a few examples which I have given in another place: see note 27.

(40) St. John v, 39.

And even when written, how was Faith ensured
While they remained in mists of doubt obscured;
Mists that, indeed, as all Church-records tell,
It took the lapse of ages to dispel?
But saying, "search the Scriptures," if we hold
That our Lord meant, assuredly, the *old*—
Does that imply that we forbid the use
Of the new Scriptures, guarded from abuse?
Quite the reverse: we hold it just and meet,
Helped by the wisdom of the Paraclete,
That Old and New should certainly be read
With the church-ordinance, but *not instead.*

All Scripture profitable is to teach,
Saint Paul declares—a text you often preach.—
Scripture, we know, is profitably read
By all where inspiration's light is shed;
By us, who in Church-inspiration see,
Or Heaven-appointed men, like Timothy.
Turn as you can the precept, and, at best,
You find that he was specially addressed:
As one in whom the Spirit was enshrined,
One for the Truth's establishment designed:
Plainly distinct from those, of whom, 'tis said,
The Bible brings destruction on their head:
For the same book, that men like him directs,
Starts heresies, and breaks them into sects.

What is the genuine word not *we* discuss,
Nor *you*: the *Church has judged* for you and us.
From spurious writings was Religion freed,
Just as they with Tradition disagreed.
And so Tradition in your faith we see,
In spite of all condemning theory.

Indeed, while other sects refuse it grace,
And deprecate its aid in every case,
With them disputing, you are even found
Plainly positioned on this Popish ground.
Thus under Church-authority, at length,
Your Rule confesses its inferior strength:
So vanishes, in one short moment lost,
Your boasted groundwork that such labor cost;
And your distinctive light we cease to see,
Gone out in Roman Catholicity.
When to this point for your existence driven,
We view the bonds of your existence riven:
So dies the hunted whale, whose mortal strife
Occurs just where he finds the air of life.
And when, at other times, you boldly try
All Church-authorization to deny
In any matter of true Christian faith,
Yielding alone to what the Bible saith;
We then may call attention to your strange
Adoption of the Popish Sabbath-change,
By which we find the old observance passed
Now to the week's *first* day, even from the *last*.
And then completely be prepared to prove
The Bible-orthodoxy of the move,—
Explaining clearly how it cannot be
Esteemed a sign of Church-authority;
And, turning to the *Text* with ready hand,
Show for the change a plain express command.
But vainly yet, I fear, the inquirer dips
For this from *Matthew* to *Apocalypse*:
And if the mandate is not clearly *there*,
It must, of course, have been received *elsewhere*;

So thus *against* the Bible you have gone;
Or, else, it serves not *by itself alone.*

Nor will appear from other points of view
Your doctrine more consistent and more true.
The various counts on which it may be tried
Sure condemnation bring on every side.
Four centuries of doubt were fully gone—
And then the church, you say, was "*Babylon*"—
Before the cautious censor would allow
All of the Testament that we have now.
No wonder, then, it often dimly shines—
This Rule of Faith *curst "Babylon" defines!*
And is it strange if men should even see
Destruction there and instability?
Luther called James's scripture "*one of straw,*"
And kicked "*the Hebrews*" from the Canon law:
These two and others, once declared profane,
And kicked out also, you kicked back again.
'Tis a tough Rule that such rough usage bore;
And ne'er was rule so rudely ruled before;
Nor very sacred seems its dubious place—
Now all of honor, now of mixed disgrace;[41]
And quite to scorn it may hereafter fall:
Some *greater Luther* may *reject it all!*

(41) Notwithstanding the 6th of the 39 *articles*, it is conceded that many parts of the New Testament were subject to the inquiry of the Church for a long period of time. Three or four centuries elapsed before the second and third Epistles of St. John were finally received as canonical, and not until the fifth century was St. Paul's to the Hebrews admitted by the Latin Church. This Epistle, the Epistle of James, and other scriptures, were rejected by Luther and other Protestants, but have been again received by the Anglicans.

Here we may note, that *our unshaken church*
Retains what scriptures ever passed her porch;
Nor vainly those long centuries she took
To judge the writings that should form the book—
Slow to refuse, indeed, or to accept
What must, for ever, be refused or kept:[42]
So different from wavering heresy,
Which cannot with one constant rule agree;
Whose newer variations are not strange;
When even its groundwork shows the curse of
    change.
    But seems your Rule more worthy to be prized,
By yet another method scrutinized?—
You hold the books of Scripture, that compose
The Testament, both old and new, as those,
The Church ne'er doubted; though you've still
    decreed,
The Faith must from the written word proceed:
So, while the Church is on the Scripture piled,
The parent seems the offspring·of the child!
It must be so: the Church compiled the Book,
Yet from the latter its existence took![43]

(42) Among the Books of Scripture finally rejected by the Church
were eight "Gospels," five "Acts of the Apostles," and three
"Revelations." Many others were also rejected, and among them
one called *the Pastor* or *Shepherd*, which the Protestant *Whiston*
calls "*an inspired book, which comes directly from the Saviour, as does
the Apocalypse.*" Those who do not receive their Rule of Faith from
the Church must, of course, see the necessity of inquiring *why* those
scriptures were rejected. See preceding note.

(43) The sixth article of Anglican doctrine affirms that "*In the
name of the Holy Scripture we do understand those canonical Books of
the Old and New Testament,* OF WHOSE AUTHORITY WAS NEVER ANY
DOUBT IN THE CHURCH."

Or we may differently still discuss
This case absurd, and, lastly, put it thus :—
In spite of the sixth article your creed
Comprises, you must yet, in truth, concede,
The Book was wanting for some hundred years :—
Show in that period *where* the Church appears,—
Or rather *how;* because Christ's Church upon
His Book, you say, depends; and there was
    none.
Christ founded it; and still you seem to see,
Without the Book that guides, it could not be.
To this conclusion, then, the question tends :—
That even before the church begins, it ends !
'Tis all a paradox, however viewed,
And only non-inquirers can delude.
You say our mysteries make faith less true;
But where's the mystery so great as you ?
    With *us*, you see, no difficulty lies :
The Church from oral teaching takes its rise.
The Book confirms our faith, but not supplies.
On spoken words—not written—was it grounded;
And so perpetuated just as founded.
The Apostolic manuscripts are lost;
Yet, safely still within the Church embossed,
The faith remains, removed from depredations
Of faithless copies, or impure translations.
It matters little was the language Greek,
Or Latin, or abstruser Shemitic
Of Holy writ, or even if it passed
Through those successively to ours at last.
A letter, word or verse of it purloined,
Or changed, or spurious words or texts subjoined

Can make with us but little difference,
Who, independent of it, have the sense.

We yet maintain that Bible-doctrine's pure;
But how can Protestants believe it sure?
You say the sacred writings now received,
Are those whose truth the Church ne'er disbelieved,
But your own reason to the Church prefer;
Because the *latter*, you have said, *may err.*
It then may err in *any way* it moves;
Even *when certain Scriptures it approves;*
And, therefore, when upon the Book you read
Depends the true construction of your creed,
The Church's sanction you ought not to take,
But should your personal inquiries make.
Yet trying if the genuine word be there,
Would leave, I fear, no *preaching* time to spare.
Luther declares, who at the endeavor sneers,
The task would take you full one hundred years.
Nay; these you want to prove it likely true,
And then as many to explore it through.
As their old worship, since the Temple fell,
Is rendered to the Jews impossible,
In your unfavored Rule of Faith we see
As evident impossibility:
A perfect Protestant there *cannot* be.[44]

(44) The history of the Anglican *Rule of Faith*—the English Bible
—is not edifying. The first was Tindal's in 1526, which was soon
condemned for its corruptions. The next was Coverdale's in 1535,
which met with no better success. In 1568 was published the celebrated BISHOPS' BIBLE, edited by Parker and the English bishops,
and which, in forty years after, we find the Bishops and clergy condemning in a petition to King James, because it "*takes from the text,
and adds to the text; it obscures and changes the meaning of the Holy
Ghost.*" The Rev. Mr. Broughton declared that it "*caused millions*

of souls to run into eternal flames." A valuable *Rule of Faith* truly! This was replaced by "King James's Bible," our present *Rule*, which, however, has been condemned by many celebrated Protestant divines. Dr. McKnight says of it, "*It is by no means such a just representation of the inspired originals as merits to be implicitly relied on for determining the controverted articles of Christian faith and for quieting the dissensions which have rent the Church.*" D'Israeli, in his *Curiosities of Literature*, under the head of *The Pearl Bible*, speaks of "*the extraordinary state of our English Bibles, which were for some time suffered to be so corrupted that no books ever yet swarmed with such innumerable errors. These errors, unquestionably, were in great part voluntary commissions, passages interpolated and meanings forged for certain purposes, sometimes to sanction the new creed of a self-hatched sect, and sometimes with an intention to destroy all scriptural authority by a confusion or an omission of texts.*" "*One Bible swarmed with six thousand faults.*" He shows that *Field*, the editor of the Pearl Bible, got a bribe of fifteen hundred pounds to change the letter w into a y, for the purpose of proving that the appointment of pastors ought to be in the hands of the people. This was done in the third verse of the sixth chapter of the Acts, where the words of the Apostles "wɪ *may appoint*" were read "ʏɪ *may appoint.*"

We read in Dr. Witham's preface to the Rheims Testament that the Greek edition of the New Testament, printed at Oxford in 1675, has given us out of divers MSS. about *twelve or thirteen thousand different readings*, as they have been numbered by a Protestant author, who published an edition of the New Testament at Amsterdam, Ex Officina Westeniana, An. 1711. This author, giving an account of the labors of the learned Dr. Mills, tells us, that out of 120 MSS. he published, An. 1707, about *thirty thousand different readings.*

In a book lately published by Mr. James Fitzjames Stephen, M.A., he puts forward various statements of some of the most celebrated Anglican divines to show their estimate of the Bible and of Biblical interpretation. The work contains his very able defence of the Revd. Rowland Williams, D.D., in the Arches' Court of Canterbury, and is worth the attention of those, who, with any sincerity, join in the daily advertised invitations of "The Mission" — "*Roman Catholics, bring your bibles, come and hear.*"

Bishop Lowth, as quoted by Mr. Stephen, tells us that the introduction of the vowel points, or the Masoretic punctuation, "is in effect an *interpretation* of the Hebrew text made by the *Jews of late ages*, probably not earlier than the *eighth century.*" He explains how the meaning of the text is determined by the *management of the points*, and states that "our public translations in the modern tongues for the use of the Church among Protestants, and so likewise of the modern Latin translations, are for the most part, close copies of the Hebrew *pointed* text, and are in reality only versions at second hand." From this it would appear that the English Bible can show, at best, only the way in which the Jews of the eighth century *considered* that they ought to read the Hebrew which was written without vowels in a kind of shorthand. Nor had they then to deal with the *original* manuscripts which dated from one to two thousand years before; and the Bishop remarks that "all writings transmitted to us like these from early times, the original copies of which have long ago perished, have suffered in their passage to us by the mistakes of many transcribers, through whose hands we have received them: errors continually accumulating in proportion to the number of transcripts, and the stream generally becoming more impure the more distant it is from the source." (pp. 48, 49, 50.) An extract from a high Anglican authority, Jeremy Taylor, shows his views on the subject of expounding Scripture : the following is a part of it :—"And since on the other side there are, in Scripture, many other mysteries and matters of question upon which there is a veil ; since there are so many copies with infinite varieties of reading ; since a various interpunction, a parenthesis, a letter, an accent, may much alter the sense ; since some places have divers literal senses, many have spiritual, mystical and allegorical meanings ; since there are so many tropes, metonymies, ironies, hyperboles, proprieties and improprieties of language, whose understanding depends upon such circumstances that it is almost impossible to know its proper interpretation now that the knowledge of such circumstances and particular stories is irrecoverably lost ; since there are some mysteries which, at the best advantage of expression, are not easy to be apprehended, and whose explanation by reason of our imperfections must needs be dark, sometimes weak, sometimes unintelligible ; and lastly, since those ordinary means of expounding Scripture, as searching the originals, conference of places, parity of reason, and analogy of faith, are all dubious, uncertain, and very fallible : he that is the wisest, and by consequence the likeliest to expound truest in all probability of reason, will be very far from confidence, because every one of these, and many more, are like so many degrees of improbability and uncertainty, all depressing our certainty of finding out truth in such mysteries and amidst so many difficulties." (pp. 105, 106.) This is a strongly drawn statement, not indeed very suggestive of hope to one who yet will not see an infallible expounder in the Church.

Mr. Stephen proves the opposition of the most distinguished

Anglican churchmen to what is called the "organic or plenary" inspiration of the Bible, and in a "summary of argument" he repeats that "Tillotson lays down the principle that you need not assume inspiration in any part of the Bible which might have been thought without inspiration. Burnet says, and Paley supports him in saying, that you are bound to agree to the Apostles' conclusions, but you are not bound to agree with their premises. Butler treats the whole question as a question of fact. Berkely admits that the Bible was not intended to be strictly accurate in circumstantials in reference to history; Paley declares that it is dangerous to make Christianity answerable for the circumstantial accuracy of the Old Testament narratives. Scott says the same thing, so does Watson. Bishop Marsh says the same thing in a stronger form, and endorses the opinion of Michaelis that *the Gospels of Luke and Mark were not inspired at all.* Horsley asserts his right to differ on all but religious subjects from St. Paul, David, or any other Scriptural writer; and Archbishop Sumner's language, and the language of Dr. Whewell, admit of no other construction than that if Science and Scripture differ, Science is right and Scripture wrong. The same view is worked out at great length by Archbishop Whateley, and Bishop Hampden declares that the language of the Bible may contain *much false moral philosophy.*" (pp. 179, 180.) Butler supposes a case of a person, ignorant of Scripture, like my "creedless man," and admits to him that "there may be mistakes of transcribers, there may be other *real* or seeming mistakes not easy to be particularly accounted for, but there are certainly no more things of this kind in the Scripture than what were to have been expected in books of such antiquity, &c." (p. 139.)

When such are the opinions of English ecclesiastics respecting the *Anglican Rule 'of Faith,* it is not surprising that it should be "*expressly denied,*" as Mr. Stephen tells us, by some of their most eminent writers in their hopelessness to maintain it against Roman Catholic argument. Mr. Stephen, however, does not find them to be happy in their choice of a substitute, when they declare that the *Apostles' Creed* is the Rule—a rule, he observes, "not said to be inspired at all—a document 'not in the Bible—a document *resting merely on tradition,* &c." (pp. 102, 103, 104.) I may add that, among difficulties suggested by himself, Mr. Stephen, alluding to a text in the Greek Testament, points out how, "according as the line in the letter Θ is present or absent, the passage becomes or ceases to be a warrant of Holy Scripture from which part of the Athanasian Creed may be proved." (p. 37).

The following will illustrate the embarrassments, or rather one class of them, by which the Rule of Faith of Anglican doctrine is beset:—the Arians deny the authenticity of a certain text of Scripture, which furnishes one of the strongest proofs in favor of the doctrine of the Trinity ; and it is admitted that the verse in question —the 7th of 1 St. John v.—though cited by some of the earliest writers, was not quoted among the Latins by St. Ambrose, nor by St. Augustine, nor by St. Leo, nor by Venerable Bede, nor, among the Greek writers, by St. Cyril of Alexandria. This important omission must be accounted for by the fact, that the verse was not found in the copies of the Bible used by them; [See Dr. Mac Evilly's Exposition]—and now we might fairly inquire, how, in the exercise of their *private judgment*, those of our Anglican brethren, who have not *thoroughly sifted every authority on the subject*, decide for the canonicity of this text, and agree to its insertion in their Testament.

We might further ask, by what means every Anglican has satisfied his *private judgment* that the genuineness of the Second Epistle of St. Peter, the Second and Third of St. John, the Epistle of St. Jude, and the Apocalypse, is not affected by their absence from the Syriac version of the Holy Writings, and on what grounds he believes *his* judgment to be superior to that of *Luther* who expunged from his "*Rule of Faith*" the Epistle of St. James and other Scriptures.

Finally we may conclude that, irrespective of the question of seeking by private interpretation to understand the Bible as it is, the period of "one hundred years" would not be too much for the *preparatory* inquiries:—1. Whether the present English Bible is *wholly*, or only *partly*, or *at all* a version of the one from which it is assumed to be translated ; whether *that* was, itself, wholly, or only partly, or at all a version of the one from which it was said to be taken, and so on to the original manuscripts of the sacred writers: 2. Whether the first Bible (the correctness of the translations being proved) ought to be considered as inspired *wholly*, or only *partly,* or *at all* ; and, 3. if inspired at all, but not wholly, what were the *precise parts* of it that were derived from the Holy Spirit. It is plain that all those investigations are, in point of fact, necessary for every person who inclines to Anglican opinions, but, as the impossibility of his achieving them is equally evident, I think I am justified in asserting that there "*cannot* be" such a thing as a "perfect Protestant" who depends on his *private judgment*, and not on the authority of the traditional Church for his *Rule of Faith*.

In my allusion to the Jews, I refer to the recognized fact, that one of the plainest proofs of the ending of the Jewish Dispensation is seen in the impossibility of complying with it, and offering sacrifice since the destruction of the Temple.

ANGLICANIA.

—

PART III.

PART III.

At first, Reformers seemed to think it clear,
As the Church erred, so Faith could disappear;
Though some would say, Reformers quite forgot
To think at all it either could or not,—
Caring but little what the Scripture showed,
And taking just for granted that it could.
There was a certain object to be gained,
And then no questioning was entertained.
From Church-restraint their aim was to get free,
And overthrow the irksome Papacy.
So they made war on Rome with little sense,
Not calculating on their foe's defence,
Who well objected that what *they* believed,
Implied that Christ, when promising, deceived.—
The Church could *not* err, if He promised right,
And should remain undimmed in mortal's sight—
For ever visible.[45]   They found a flaw
In the attack, but would not quite withdraw.
If they retreated, it was but to trace
Their operations from another base.
"Though the *Church* erred," as they would *now*
       expound,
"The *faith* was always *somewhere* to be found

(45) The doctrines of visibility and invisibility are among the
contradictions now held simultaneously in the Church of England.
For an account of some of the great divisions and subdivisions of the
Establishment see the Edinburgh Review, October 1853.j
5

"In just succession, though, it might be true,
"At times appearing only in a few."
So had Christ's promises not *wholly* failed;
And not *completely* had hell's gates prevailed.
There was succession out of Rome, no doubt,
Though hard to find; but yet it *was* made out,
They say: then, Anglicans, declare *through whom*
Has come the form of faith that you assume ;—
But mind that, in your long ancestral list,
No single individual be missed;
And it is quite as necessary too
To prove that each believed the same as you;
Or as your Church, at least, pretends to do:
For if the faith of all was not the same,
No genuine succession can you claim;
And, like the achievement of a north-west cruise,
You find a passage which you cannot use.
'Tis not enough in *some* points to agree;
Else simple Deism would bar heresy.
And if the Faith's transmitters disagreed,
Then did the Faith through heresy proceed;
And hell helped Heaven to hand it down indeed!
But 't were absurd to think it could be so,
And that THE FAITH through differing Creeds
    could flow.
When all the links are not the same to view,
The chain must be rejected as not true;
And let us see how far may this apply
To the precursors on whom you rely,
As the blest line in which, outside of Rome,
Christ's doctrine to Reformers must have come.—

Huss would the Pope's supremacy deride:
A Protestant in little else beside.
Wickliffe with Luther 'gainst the Pope agrees;
And both in other points are Manichees;
Or rather in their doctrines we can see
A blacker type of Manes' blasphemy:
For he would have two lords of Good and Evil;
And they in one would find both God and devil.[46]

In the Waldenses let succession rest!
(Still hatred to the Pope appears your test.)
What if their founders never yet rebelled
Against the Sacraments the Papists held!
Nor even against the Pope until by him expelled!
Still less like yours did their poor church appear,
When keeping from the *loaves and fishes* clear;

(46) Wickliffe taught that God was the author of sin; as did
Luther and other chiefs of the Reformation. Wickliffe says in his
Trialog (L. 3. c. 4.) that *God approves of our sinning, that he neces-
sitates our sinning, &c.* The Calvinist Jurieu upbraided the
Lutherans with the doctrine of their founder who declared, that
*Judas could not avoid betraying his master; that every thing good and
bad among men happens by necessity; that God makes men incur
damnation by necessity; that the adultery of David was no less the
work of God than the conversion of St. Paul, &c.* (Bossuet, Var.
Addition au Livre xiv. n. 2.) But Jurieu ought to have taken the
beam out of his own eye; for *Calvin* said that *Adam could not avoid
his fall; for God ordained it, as it was comprised in his secret design;
that the reprobate are inexcusable, although they cannot avoid the
necessity of sinning, and that necessity occurs by the command of
God; that God speaks to them, but to make them deaf; that he puts
the light before their eyes, but to blind them; that he sends them his
divine word, but to make them more insensible; that he gives them
remedies, but not to cure them.* (Ibid. n. 3.) However, Jurieu
admitted that Reformers in general taught that, *God impelled the
wicked to enormous crimes,* and Bossuet remarks—"*Sans contestation
es chefs des deux parties de la réforme, Luther et Melancton d'un
côté, Calvin et Beze de l'autre, les mâitres et les disciples sont également
convaincus de manichéisme et d'impisté.*" (Ibid.)

Nor do your preachers seem like them to prize,
With feet unshod, a squalid monkish guise.
Widely from you in points they differed thus;
And so in others from both you and us :—
A sinless layman could perform as priest;
And when a priest transgressed his functions ceased:
If *you* taught this of priests that plainly sinned,
Soon would your MISSION's truthless stock be
    thinned.
  But then the Albigenses, we must grant,
Beyond comparing were more Protestant.
"No Transubstantiation *there*;" you cry :—
'Tis true; for *Incarnation* they deny.
Then the old Testament; they styled it *all*,
As you an *ample part*, apocryphal;
And baptism, as a humbug, they despised:
A sacrament with you but little prized.
A dreadful sin in marriage they would see;
 . While you at least abate its sanctity.
They quite forbade it; but your kinder course,
Is to permit it, subject to divorce.
Thus we admit your very great degree
Of likeness to the Albi-manichee;
Yet is the likeness still too incomplete:
The Albigenses would allow *no meat;*
And when the Faith keeps not the stomach full,
It is rank heresy with friend, John Bull.[47]

' (47) For the doctrines held by the Waldenses and Albigenses see
Bossuet's Variations, 11th *Book,* where the Manicheism of the latter
and the Donatism of the former are clearly proved. The heresies,
that forbade meat as food, and also prohibited marriage, were foretold by St. Paul in his first epistle to Timothy (iv. 3.) It is merely
puerile to say that the Catholic Church denies the use of meat,
because she enjoins fasting at certain times. The Anglican, who

Now single writers stop ancestral gaps,
As Protestants on single points perhaps.
Any break off in faith, and you insist
On placing each demurrer in your list.
What they all *were*, it matters scarce a groat;
'Tis quite enough to know what they *were not*.

believes himself to be emancipated from this ordinance, and who
applies St. Paul's prophecy to her, had better look to his own *Book
of Common Prayer*, where he will find fasting and abstinence as
clearly prescribed as in the Catholic Church:—See the following
"*table of Vigils, Fasts, and Days of Abstinence to be observed in the
year:*—

"The Evens, or vigils before the nativity of our Lord. The
Purification of the Blessed Virgin Mary. The Annunciation of the
Blessed Virgin. Easter Day. Ascension Day. Pentecost. St.
Mathias. S. John Baptist. S. Peter. S. James. S. Bartholomew.
S. Matthew. S. Simon and Jude. S. Andrew. S. Thomas. All Saints.

"Note. That if any of these feast days fall upon a Monday, then
the Vigil or Fast-day shall be kept upon the Saturday and not upon
the Sunday next before it."

The days of fasting and abstinence (not vigils) are:—"1. The forty
days of Lent.

2. The Ember-days at the four seasons, being the Wednesday,
Friday and Saturday after the first Sunday in Lent; the feast of
Pentecost; September 14th; December 13th.

3. The three Rogation-days, being the Monday, Tuesday, and
Wednesday before Holy Thursday, or the Ascension of our Lord.

4. All the Fridays in the year, except Christmas Day."

The Feasts comprise many Saints' days besides those mentioned
above, and include the Sundays which are not distinguished as of
superior sanctity. As to marriage, our Church, far from forbidding
it, even makes it a sacrament. Priests are required by a Rule of
discipline to take a vow of celibacy, as the Church believes their
cares will be made less worldly thereby. Others who solemnly make
similar vows are required to keep them. Though a point of Faith
could not be changed, the rule of the priests' celibacy could, though
it, probably, never will. If Anglicans do not forbid marriage like
the Manicheans, they certainly do not encourage it, as is proved
by their *Divorce Court*, the greatest scandal of the nineteenth
century.

Thus on the SUPPER, Berenger alone
Disputed; and you claim him for your own;[48]
And Arian Claude is in your series placed:
As Protestant, as an iconoclast.

Passing long ages, where the unlucky plant
Of faith appears not, come to Vigilant.
He, it is said, would saintly intercession
Deride, and therefore answers your progression.
Still is your boast one single heretic,
Though far less Protestant than Catholic;
And the quite early church was surely dim,
Whose visibility was all in him,
And scarcely worth its site upon the rock,
When one lone man was bishop, priest and flock.[49]

(48) Though Berenger disputed the Real Presence, and is therefore
claimed as one of the Protestant *links* to the Apostles, still that
doctrine is not so completely negatived in their Church as Anglicans
commonly believe. We have high Anglican authorities in favor of
it, and the *Times* paper, in an article that defines it as a *point which
defies human scrutiny*, rightly declares that there will be differences
regarding it "*as long*," it says, "*as our Church is a Church.*" A
large portion of the article, in which that very safe prediction appears,
will be found in a note to Part IV.

(49) As in various other points, the Anglican Church is not by any
means so opposed to Catholic doctrine regarding the interference of
Saints between God and man, as many of its members imagine.
The Catholics ask the Saints to intercede with God for his mercy.
They also beseech God to grant them the assistance of the angels to
"defend their lives here on earth." (See collect, Feast of S.
Michael.) They are joined by the Anglicans in the latter part of the
doctrine, which shows that benefits may come directly from the
angels, but are opposed in the first part, where the required benefits
are shown to be expected directly from God. How those who
dispute this can admit the other, is rather difficult to be understood.
The Anglican collect on the Feast of *Saint Michael and all Angels*
is as follows:—

Still higher up the path of time you press
For older indications of your race.
You find Aërius; but let us see
How far a genuine Protestant was he:—
So far, at least, as never to be led
To offer up his masses for the dead.
And was he not of popes the certain foe?
Yes: but he was an *Arian* we know,
Denying the divinity of Christ;—
No matter! to your lineage have him spliced.[50]

"O everlasting God, who hast ordained and constituted the
services of angels and men in a wonderful order; mercifully grant
that as thy holy angels always do thee service in Heaven; so by thy
appointment they may succour and defend us on earth, through Jesus
Christ, our Lord. Amen."

(50) Praying for the dead is one of those points in which there
does not appear to be that difference between the Catholic Church
and Anglicanism that the adherents of the latter generally seem to
think. We see this proved by various Anglican authorities, and by
the following judgment of *the Court of Arches*, quoted by the Rev.
Mr. Bennett, Vicar of Frome, in his defence of that practice.
"Prayer for the dead is not contrary to the articles and canons of
the church of England. It was generally practised by the Christians
of the most early ages, who prayed that the souls of the dead may
have rest and quiet between death and the resurrection; and that at
the last day they may receive their perfect consummation and bliss."
The *Compass* of June 21, 1861, in an article on the subject of
prayers for the dead, and alluding to a writer who signs himself "a
Beneficed Priest," says—"He refers to the case of Breeks *v.*
Woolfrey, which establishes that by the law of the Court of Arches,
which is the law of the Church of England, prayers for the dead are
authorized, and inscriptions on tombstones inculcating that doctrine
are legal."

I may remark that in English Universities there is no scruple
about making use of endowments given for the purpose of having
masses offered for the souls of their founders. (Edinburgh Review,
July, 1852, pp. 249, 250.) Who reads the masses I am unable to
say; but the bequests are enjoyed.

I will give one more instance of identity between our faith and

Thus you construct a false ancestral tree
By odds and ends of similarity;
And to illustrate your strange use of those,
We may, perhaps, the following case suppose;—
Where some old merchant, vain and overgrown
In wealth, retired from business and the town,
And thousands spending on a country seat,
Might yet not think his happiness complete,
If failing with his riches to combine
The fancied eclat of an ancient line;
Quaintly desiring that his best renown
Were thought his ancestors', and not his own.—
Nor is it among men so rare a course
To boast more of their luck than their own force;
And the old worthy of our theme may be
So plied by this o'erpowering vanity,
That, crazed upon the point, he tries to trace
A written pedigree to prove his race;
And, wishing still more showy proofs to add,
(For the most silly are the vain gone mad)
He, for the object nearest to his heart,
Spends tens or hundreds at the picture mart,
And sticks a lot of portraits on his walls
In drawing-rooms and libraries and halls.
Then here behold the various-vested squires!
This is his father: those, more distant sires.
In each old likeness he would make us see
Some mark that gives it to his ancestry.

Anglicanism, though it is commonly *ignored* by those who *profess* the
latter: that is, the *power of absolution by the priest*, which is shown
by the service for the sick in the *Book of Common Prayer*. This
simultaneous admission and denial of various points of doctrine is
the most remarkable part of the Anglican puzzle.

An ancestor in this the *eyes* disclose :—
In that we catch another by the *nose;*
Next from a *mouth* the kin must be inferred,
And there again it hangs upon a *beard.*
Such are the data given to define
The truth of the paternal painted line—
By general likeness we must not compare,
But by resemblances found here and there—
And, though this face, perhaps, was Smith's or
    Brown's,
That Jones's, and that other, Robinson's,
All for his ancestors friend Green secures :
His proofs of kindred—just the same as yours.
  Now back to Peter for three hundred years
No antipapal ancestor appears.
And the Reformers seemed to understand
The strange precursors that they took in hand;
For we may well remark, they never rose
Simply to teach any whole creed of those.
None showed a disposition to concede
To them the *pure* conveyance of the creed.
It came through them, but not in a condition
Approved of by reformers for transmission,
Who tried not, then, this *creed's dissemination,*
But said they sought the *church's reformation.*
They spoke of Rome: the *church* was plainly
    there;
But *truth* and the *succession* were elsewhere.
Here is a gospel paradox disclosed :
'Twas not the faithful that the church composed.
The faithful were *without the church;* and yet
Within it only are the faithful met :

Yet those within were faithless; and the rest,
Outside, were heretics quite manifest.
Faithful, and still in faithlessness depraved,
Both parties should at once be damned and
    saved.
What's to be done, then, between bale and glory?
Never was such a want for *Purgatory!*

Though Roman faith reformers all decried,
That Rome's was still the church was not denied.
Luther proclaimed, amid his deepest rage,
Hers was indeed the church in every age;
Which, though demanding his reforms, forsooth,
Was yet "the pillar and the ground of truth.
"In her miraculously must endure
"Each sacrament; for Heavenly Powers assure:—
"By her, in various idioms undepraved,
"Miraculously too, God's Book is saved:—
"Vocation of the priest and ordination,
"In the last agony true consolation
"Are hers," he says; "and, spite of any taints,
"She is, undoubtedly, the home of Saints;
"And, if, in certain points, she yet rebels,
"Within her, still, the Holy Spirit dwells."[51]

Thus against Rome the Reformation stormed;
Rome's was the church, and that should be
    reformed.
So an eccentric zeal was then exerted
To have the church of Christ to Christ converted.

(51) These sentiments of the inexplicable Luther regarding the
Church of Rome are contained in his treatise on the Private Mass.
This was written many years after his secession, and four years after
the confession of Augsburg. (Bossuet, Var. l. iii, n. 60.)

Unless the church, indeed, was truly here,
It did unquestionably disappear.
And now in sober seriousness declare,
How can *succession* be produced elsewhere?
From Luther to Aërius we see
But one sole trace of general unity,
Shown in the point which goes to supersede
One regent for the universal creed.—
Say now that this suffices;—even so,
Not to the needful limits can you go.
Though taking for succession's blest degrees
Waldenses, Albigenses, Manichees
And Arians, as tracing you ascend,
This side of the Apostles you must end.
The utmost point unable to attain,
By passing Luther you but little gain;
For when your line is still too short, we know
It does not matter then *how much* 'tis so.
Yet farther back than Luther it were wrong
To grant the line *unbroken* short or long.
By faulty steps you try to rise in vain,
And not by one continuous even plain.
Your best procession's marks are only found
Where distant schisms sunk in unsolid ground;
And to trace back by signs so far apart
To the desired commencement, mocks your art:
So following a half-dried river's course
By separate pools, we come to no true source.
    But now suppose that the reformers proved
Succession, and each obstacle removed;
Quære—to *which* reformer of them all
Did the succession veritably fall?

Scarce better with each other they agreed,
Than any of them with the Papists' Creed.
Luther, who Zuinglius in hell would burn,
Was as devoutly prayed for in return.
With Carlostadt, in fellowship as strange,
He would the worst anathemas exchange.
Calvin would Bucer's gospel shufflings hoot,
And branded Osiander as a brute.
So zealous were they, when their blood was up,
They hit each other striking at the Pope;
Or, like o'er-anxious curs that run to bite,
They jostled, and began themselves to fight.
Now a reformer dies; and then another
Swears 'twas the devil seized his wretched brother.
Against the Pope they used the devil first;
But soon would have each other with him curst.
At length they took for damning such a zest,
They scarcely let him, the poor devil, rest;
But kept him going, while they cursed and swore,
With dexterous sectarian battledoor.
The game is not the flying fiend to shun,
But pass him round and round from one to one.
So while against the Pope their curses rise,
Between themselves foul malediction flies.
It is all tumult and perpetual din:
A war of sin with Heaven, and sin with sin.
Such imprecations fall in fiery showers!
Such dread consignments to the infernal powers!
We think we hear Hell's doors for ever slamming,
While sect keeps sect, and doctrine doctrine
        damning.

Into such dire confusion they were plunged;
Now was a tenet added, now expunged.
Here a "*Confession*" the true faith decrees,
And with one quite as truthful disagrees.
Now a reformer settles his last will,
Then abrogates it all by codicil.
He for a point to-day would lose his life,
And may to-morrow yield it without strife.
Now there is something said the Pope to teaze,
And then unsaid the Emperor to please.
Religion moves them, but *against* its force
They plainly sail by changeful tacking course;
Or, like unskilful painters, seek renown,
By constant brightening up and toning down:
So *variable* is each gospel plan,
Except THE ONE that *did not come from man.*[52]

(52) For the disputes between Reformers, and the differences in
their own tenets at different times, I must refer to Bossuet; but to
show that their disputes were not unimportant, I will give a few
specimens taken from his " *Variations,*" of the manner in which they
used to express their opinions of each other. Luther writes of
Zuinglius, " *How can one be silent when such people trouble our churches
and our authority?*" and concludes by saying that *there is no middle
course;* that *either he or they are ministers of Satan.* (Var. l. ii.
n. 28.) He also said of the Zuinglians that, *he considered them
heretics and distant from the church of God* (Ibid, l. vi. n. 40.) In an
epistle to the librarian at Zurich he denounced the Zuinglians *as
men damned, who drew others into hell* (Ibid, n. 13.) At another time
he put Zuinglius and Oecolampadius on a level with Arius, and with
*the idolators who make an idol of their own thoughts, and adore them
in contempt of the word of God;* and afterwards he treated them as
*madmen, blasphemers, damned people, for whom it was no longer
permitted to pray,* and protested against any further intercourse with
them, unless they admitted that *the bread of the Eucharist was the
true natural body of our Lord.* (Ibid, n. 14.) The Zuinglians were
not slow in retorting, calling Luther *the new Antichrist* (Ibid, n. 15.)

The solemn signs are worth considering
That proved the Reformation's heavenly spring!
There, always, is some dreadful wonder going :—
One day the Tiber takes to overflowing :

and we may discover *Calvin's* opinion of the Lutherans, and their hostility to him, when he says that *he cannot comprehend why they attack him more violently than the others unless it is that Sutan, of whom they are the vile slaves, excite them the more against him, as his works are more useful for the good of the church* (Ib. l. ix. n. 82.) Calvin's opinion of Bucer is expressed in milder terms, but is scarce more complimentary to one of the *leaders* of the Reformation. In pointing out an obscurity in a profession of faith, he would say that, *there could not be any thing more embarrassing, more obscure, more ambiguous, more tortuous in Bucer himself.* (Ib. l. iv. n. 25.) Now for Calvin's opinion of Osiander, another of the great lights of the Reformation, and head of the church of Nuremberg : he blames him for his drunken blasphemies in calling himself *the son of the Living God, &c.* and designates him *a brute, and a ferocious beast, whose profane spirit and infamous manners he detested from the day he first saw him.* (Ib. l. viii. n. 12.) Melancthon, although he often praised Osiander, frequently censured him for his reveries, excesses, monstrous opinions and the *new opinions* he brought into the church. (Ib. n. 13.) Calvin also exclaimed against Melancthon's equivocations (Ib. l. iv. n. 25.) Melancthon described Carlostadt, another of the pillars, as *brutal, ignorant, without piety, without humanity, and more of a Jew than a Christian.* (Ib. l. ii. n. 7.) Luther declared that he retained the elevation of the Host to annoy Carlostadt ; (a most pious motive truly) and *"for fear that it might appear to me that we learned any thing from the devil"* (Ib. l. ii. n. 10.) and when Luther and Carlostadt met at Jena, they parted with a challenge, and expressions such as—*"I wish I saw you on the wheel." "That you may break your neck before you leave the town,"* &c. Carlostadt subsequently got Luther pelted with stones and dirt on his entry into Orlemunde (Ib. l. ii. n. 11.) Such were the Apostles of the Reformation! Bucer writes of them all to Calvin, alluding to the victories of Charles V. *"God has punished us for the injuries we have done to his name by our so long and pernicious hypocrisy."* (Ib. l. v. n. 14.) How well would seem to apply the *third chapter of James* to those *"many masters"* of the Reformation, whose *"bitter zeal and contentions"* are of the wisdom that *"descendeth not from above, but is earthly, sensual, devilish!"* And the Epistle of St. Jude, who calls

Then is a calf produced with double head,
Or mule unnaturally "brought to bed :"
As if the creed, now coming on the earth,
Was best betokened by some monstrous birth.
Melancthon, famous at a horoscope,
Read in the stars the ruin of the Pope :
Luther foretold his fall, and various fools
Of prophecy; yet o'er the church he rules,
In spite of calves, reformers, stars and mules.[53]
    Who doubts with gospel augury to find
A christian and a heathen heaven combined ?—
Where equal glories, Zuinglius declared,
By *Peter* and the *Scipios* are shared ;—
Where Moses stands with Numa edified,
While Paul and Cato argue suicide ;—
Where *Christ—the second Adam—*is allowed
An equal place among the illustrious crowd ;
Of whom some Jove, and some Jehovah bless,
For undistinguished seats of happiness ! [54]

such men (v. 13.) "*Raging waves of the sea foaming out their own confusion; wandering stars,*" &c. And these are the *mockers* who *separate themselves.* (Ib. 18, 19.)

(53) For the signs and prodigies which the reformers regarded as foretokening the fall of the Papacy, see *Bossuet's Variations*, l. v. n. 34. In the same section will be found, the account of Melancthon's fright at the *extremely northern position of a comet*, and his joy at the slow progress made in the disputations at Augsburgh, because "*the astrologers predict that the stars will be more propitious for ecclesiastical disputes towards autumn.*" Thus was AUGURY introduced into Christianity, and was, perhaps, as valuable an element as any other proper to the Reformation.

(54) Zuinglius, in his confession, addressed to Francis I. said that he must hope to see in Heaven every *holy, virtuous, courageous and*

'Tis worth considering the sources too
From which reformers inspiration drew.
When with a spirit Zuinglius conferred,
He then was taught how Roman doctrine erred :
Perhaps from sleep, or darkness of the night,
He could not catch the color of the sprite ;
So *we* have leave to think it black or white.
But in the case of Luther, wide awake,
The lad he saw was black, and no mistake !
Luther describes his frequent disputation
With this great genius of the Reformation.
He tells how in each argument he fretted ;
How his heart beat, and how he shook and sweated
At the hard task of taking his degree
In demoniacal theology.[55]

*faithful man since the commencement of the world. He instanced
the two Adams, the redeemed and the Redeemer;* and repeated a list
of Prophets, Christian Saints, and heathen worthies and demigods,
including Numa, the founder of Roman heathenism, Theseus and
Hercules, who were, themselves, the objects of worship, Cato the
suicide, &c. &c. (Bossuet, Var. l. ii. n. 19.) Such was the company
among whom was placed the Redeemer, as the second Adam. This
fearful blasphemy throws the *augury* of Melancthon into the shade.

(55) Zuinglius derived his chief argument against the Real
Presence from a spirit that appeared to him in a dream, but he could
not say whether it was black or white (Var. l. ii. n. 27.) Luther, in
his book on the Private Mass, describes his frequent conferences
with the devil; who, after long disputing, convinced him that it
ought to be abolished. He describes his sensations during the
interviews—his terror, his perspiring, his trembling, his terrible
heart-beats, &c. "I then perceived," said he, "how it is that people
die suddenly towards the morning. It is because the devil can
strangle human beings," &c. Bossuet remarks, "Dieu, pour la
confusion, on plutôt pour la conversion des ennemis de l'Eglise, ait
permis que Luther tombât dans un assez grand aveuglement pour
avouer, non pas qu'il ait été souvent tourmenté par le demon, ce que

But not thus always were those worthies friends:
At times the hotter of the two offends,
And on poor Luther would his anger vent,
Though without proper cause of discontent;
As Luther could not, for his very life,
See how his conduct laid the grounds of strife:—
At least in this wise the blasphemer prayed,
And showed his right to call for Heavenly aid.
With Zuinglius the demon's mood was level,
But Luther found him quite a dangerous devil.[56]

Great Heaven! Are those the men that would
    inveigh
Against the church of Christ as "gone astray,"
And then proclaim that even to them the Lord
Consigned the restoration of His word?
And you, who follow them, how can you see
Truth in their demons, signs and augury—
Their outrages of blasphemy and pride—
Their jealousies and hate on every side—
Their dire assemblies and their disputations—
All contradictions and equivocations?

pouvait lui être commun avec plusiers saints; mais, ce que lui est
particulier, qu'il ait été converti par ses soins, et que l'esprit de
mensonge ait été son maître dans un des principaux points de sa
Réforme." He continues, "Si la chose est veritable, quelle horreur
d'avoir un tel maître? Si Luther se l'est imaginée, de quelles
illusions, et de quelles noires pensées avait-il l'esprit rempli? Et s'il
l'a inventée, de quelle triste aventure se fait-il honneur? (Var.
l. iv. n. 17.)

(56) For Luther's memorable *prayer*, where he complained that
the devil, *whom he never offended*, tormented him *without right or
reason*, see Bossuet, Var. l. vi. n. 17. He at the same time exclaimed
against the *Pope* and the *Grand Turk*; and he could attribute the
hostility of all three only to his *belief in the Trinity!*
6

Can you imagine that the Faith came through
This ever-changing and contentious crew,
Whose feet in gospel peace were never shod,[57]
But scattered up foul discord where they trod;
And who, for the attainment of their end,
Would each opposing fence of virtue rend?—
Their doctrine now would insurrection bring
Against priest, bishop, magistrate and king.
Against the *people* next the fiat's gone—
To slay the rebels, and not pardon one.
From marriage-bonds a fresh caprice sets free,
Or adds new fetters in polygamy
Among those mockers, whose Procrustean wit
To their own passions made the Gospel fit![58]

(57) Eph. vi. 15.

(58) For the doctrine imputed to Wickliffe : *that a king ceased to be a king on the commission of a mortal sin, and that an old woman could command a king to give up to her his throne, if she was more virtuous or better than he*—see Bossuet, Var. l. xi. n. 156. Wickliffe and the Waldenses equally believed that a priest in the state of sin lost the power of dispensing the sacraments (Var. l. xi. nn. 87. 154.) The levelling tendencies of Calvinism have been always apparent. Luther, striving to excite the Smalcaldic League to arms, exclaims, that if any one in the attack on the ferocious beast (the Pope) *is killed before he can give the beast a mortal blow, he can have only one cause of regret—that is, that he had not buried his knife in his heart.* Luther then makes known his doctrine regarding every one, even *kings*, who, differing in opinions from him, would defend the Pope, and says *that they ought to be treated like the soldiers of a chief of brigands, &c.* (Var. l. viii. n. 1.) In the war of the Anabaptist peasants against their princes, Luther wrote to the latter, saying that the people *could not, would not and ought not to suffer any longer as they did.* In a subsequent epistle he excited the princes *to exterminate the wretches without pity*, who did not profit by his advice. Then followed the war which cost Germany so much blood; and so

Can you believe, then, that the Lord made these
More blest than Arians or Manichees;
Whose older Reformations you and we
Have equally condemned for heresy?
'Twere well besides to ponder on the fact;
That in all ages each reforming act,
Which brought the charge of schism to be incurred,
Was done by *Reason* that to *Faith* demurred.
Some cannot see how Bad were made with Good,
And schismatize to have it *understood:*
Some, for the Trinity, they can't conceive,
Make one we might *more easily* believe:
Others object to Christ's corporeal pains,
And by a phantom heresy *explains*;

matters went on until the dispute with the sacramentaries kindled a
new flame. (Var. l. ii. n. 12.)

In the scandalous sermon of our great reformer on marriage,
preached at Wittemburg, the following sentence occurs, "*At first,
however, the husband must bring his wife before the church, and
admonish her two or three times, then repudiate her, and take Esther
in place of Vasti.*" See Var. l. vi. n. 11, where the novel cause of
divorce in this manner will be found. A dispensation for polygamy
was granted by the Reformers to Philip, Landgrave of Hesse, who
was permitted to have a second wife along with the Landgravine, *on
condition of its being kept secret.* The Landgrave, in applying for
the dispensation, said that *he knew* that Luther and Melancthon
advised the King of England not to break his marriage with the
queen, but to take *another wife along with her,* and among the induce-
ments offered for their compliance with the Landgrave's application
were the grants of *monasterial properties or any reasonable favors of
that kind.* The dispensation was signed by Luther, Melancthon,
Bucer and others. (Var. l. vi.)

We need not go to the Mormons to show that polygamous tendencies still exist among Reformers. In a petition to the House of
Commons permission for a plurality of wives is prayed for by Bible-
interpreting Protestants of Dundee, who believe it to be "in accord-
ance to the word of God." See report of Mr. Lygon's speech in the
Times of April 18, 1861.

And you at Transubstantiation rail,
When, thus, gross reasonings o'er faith prevail.
  So heresy 'mong Christians ever slid,
The faith of some great mystery to rid.
'Twas thought Religion, from the pressure freed,
Would to a more exalted place succeed;
But, like "the mercury," relieved of weight,
She only fell into a lower state.
  Where men denounce the faith of Rome we
      trace
Her equal libellers in every case:
As Protestants—so Arians abused;
And Manicheans in like style accused.
Rome was "idolatrous" in *every* schism:
The Pope, in foul religious despotism,
Was "Anti-christ;" and *papal* Rome, upon
Her seven hills, was plainly "Babylon."
This bright idea did not rise with you:
In previous heretics it flourished too,
Showing a kindred mark in all the crew;
Who, in each war they separately make,
Thus from one armory their weapons take.
  Yet the "Reformers'" movement was impressed
With traits distinguishing it from the rest;
For Schism selected then no favoured man,
But called up competition for the plan—
Rome-fettered doctrine boldly to set free
In the Augustan age of heresy.
And so Heresiarchs, who rose before
But singly, now came forward by the score,
To change the faith of Rome with one intent,
While in their plans of change all different.

And though their works combined were not so
    great
As single heresies of older date,
Still wide enough, from each erected head,
The scattered poison of the Hydra spread.
We must admit, however ill-advised
The measure was, it still was largely prized;
And not the less because it did begin
From even an insensate origin.
The dreamy band of Faith's epitomists
Walked with the sureness of somnambulists,
And, while no sense directed foot or hand,
Placed heresy upon a lofty stand.

    Plainly, indeed, it may at once be seen
How schism could so successful then have been;
When to a well-known fact we must agree—
From time to time some winning phantasy,
Charm of a period, but the sure surprise
Of after ages, will among men rise:
As if the pent up nonsense of mankind
In bursts, at intervals, relief must find:
Uncertain in the times it may escape;
And when it does, uncertain in what shape.
As with volcanos: now hot lavas run:
With ashy clouds they next obscure the sun:
Again 'tis volleyed stones that from them rise;
Or with innocuous smoke they fill the skies.
And, midst the whims that many an age delude,
Some bad, perhaps some harmless, but none good,
The Reformation on a level seems
With *tulip-manias* and *south-sea schemes;* [59]

(59) The *Tulipomania*, which commenced in Holland about the

The mania just being *then* in *schism*,
As now in *"volunteers"* or *spiritualism*.
  Or some might say, the mode was more unblest
In which the wild "Reform" of faith progressed;
And that it, certainly, did not *commence*
From general spontaneous fault of sense;
But that the foul and widely spreading blight
Arose from, simply, individual spite—
The spite of clever men, who spread the bane
Of folly, till they grew, themselves, insane.
A leader's genius, it is well allowed,
Will even raise a mania in a crowd,
And may, itself, when in a fevered state,
To plain insanity degenerate:
So the Reformers' hate of *him who ruled*,
To vex him, would have all the world befooled,
Till the strong poison, that made millions rave,
At length affected even them who gave;
And with mad speed the hate of Popery sped,
When all were mad—the leaders and the led.
  But still no matter how unsound the way
In which the Reformation gained its sway:
Supposing that, indeed, by fury blind
It made its total progress through mankind,
And, as an entity, is frail and mixed,
Still, as a severance, it seems well fixed.
We can't deny that though the work was wrong,
It, notwithstanding, has continued long:
Yet, while there's danger in o'erleaning walls,
Not every "hanging tower" quickly falls.

year 1634 and the English *south sea scheme* of the last century are
well known.

The schism seemed dearest to the misty north,
Whence came the Vandal, Goth and Saxon
    forth—
The ancient foes of all enlightened worth;
Where the gross blood of rugged men agrees
With the thick tarry juices of their trees.
Little exalted in those tribes we find,
Though rich in vulgar attributes of mind,
For the exploits of mean ambition fit,
And prosperous according to their wit.
Weakly with them took art and science root;
And faith grew stunted, yielding worthless fruit
In the bleak climes whose influence affects
All from the plant's low life to intellects.
Among the winds and mists and snows and rains
The sense of beauty least of all obtains.
How little in those regions are made known
The thoughts of genius, visible in stone!
Nor more than sculpture, does the painter's art
In fancy's silent language move the heart;
And if belief in Christ has there survived,
'Tis of its fairest features still deprived—
Those various means by his true doctrine given,
To reconcile the sinful soul with Heaven.
   Man, whose true home was Paradise, transforms
In burning tracts, and lands of icy storms;
And as man alters it is nothing strange,
That first his mind betrays the evil change,
And in rude northern regions testifies
The wintry aspect of the earth and skies.
'Tis plain that gloomy nature's constant frown
Repels man's aspirations to earth down;

And then, while lust and gross ambition thrive,
Art and Religion scarcely keep alive.
Though sown with care, we see the tender seeds
But feebly struggling among native weeds.
Nor by strange seeds can any human toil,
Quite change the natural herbage of the soil.
When that returns is but a point of years,
And when the flowery garden disappears.

The savage worship of the northern brood
Had little taste for sacramental food.
Slow in conversion, the dull race repined
Still for the impure doctrine they resigned.
The mysteries, that Christian faith contains,
Were too etherial for their plodding brains;
And reformation could not fail to please,
Which neared their old religion some degrees:
For Christianity was by it sued,
To be as little Christian as it could.

So mysteries of faith were soon denied,
And Christian checks on passion thrown aside.
"Good works" to the old Pagan zero fell,
As not assisting in the strife with hell.
From fasts and penance then, *de facto*, freed,
Men half restored the liberal Pagan creed;
And Odin's stubborn sons were glad to cope
On equal terms with Council and with Pope.
As Christian doctrine thus got half cashiered,
The genius of the clime and race appeared;
And, viewed with Rome, the grossness of the north,
In every age, stood prominently forth:
Its Heathenism was grosser and more free,
And so is now its Christianity.

Before it reached its full ascendant state,
Reform in England met with varied fate;
Where, truly, did Religion long prevail
According to a royal " sliding scale."
Loyally pious, that distinguished land
Received its doctrine from the monarch's hand.[60]
In certain reigns rank Popish faith the craze is;
In others, the Reformed in various phases.
'Tis now three sacraments, then only two:
Reform got stingy as it greater grew.
Again we find restored the ancient seven,
But *two*—the final contract made with heaven.[61]

(60) Though there may be "no royal road to geometry" the people of England seem to think that at least the road to Heaven is under the jurisdiction of their monarchs. During the progress of the Reformation the question with them seemed to be, not what was right, but what the Sovereign desired. This pliancy of English faith was well understood by Burnet, who remarks that if a catholic had succeeded Elizabeth on the throne, the clergy would, probably, have turned *about again to the old superstitions as nimbly as they had done before in Queen Mary's days.* (History of the Reformation, Bohn's Edition 8vo, 1857, p. 579.)

As a proof of the spell that royalty still holds over the Anglican, may be adduced a sermon on Prince Albert's visit to Liverpool by, I believe, a preacher of rather extended anti-popish fame. The sermon was printed and was entitled "*every eye shall see him; or Prince Albert's visit to Liverpool used in illustration of the second coming of Christ*," and by changing the word "*King*" into *Prince* the language of scripture, proclaiming the coming of the Lord, was travestied in the sermon. (See Edinburgh Review, No. 200, p. 292.)

(61) For the articles of the Reformed Religion under Henry VIII, see Burnet pp. 159, 160: also pp. 211, 212, where Henry's return to the *seven* sacraments will be found. For those under Edward VI, see the same; pp. 413, 414. Burnet proves (pp. 766, 767, 768.) that those articles were "*promulgated only by the King's authority*," and were never offered to convocation; nor can Burnet settle who were their real authors (p. 413.) Thus was the entire code of English

Whether the Reformation lost or gained,
A cruel character was well maintained
In all the efforts of the English nation
For or against the faith's regeneration;
And as John Bull's unlucky faith kept turning,
His zeal for truth kept hanging, racking, burning.
By those strong means at Henry's blest command
The Reformation prospered in the land;
But in young Edward's time 'twas not so dire,
Though heresy was still expelled by fire.
Cranmer, on gospel purity intent,
Gave to the flames the maniac *Joan of Kent*,
And did an equal martyrdom obtain
For his own saintship in Queen Mary's reign.
Thus while John Bull his differing martyrs fried,
And roasted turning faith on every side,
Ireland's true martyrs, thank the heavenly powers,
All died for *one* fixed faith—*and that was ours.*[62]

faith established by a youth of 15, as head of the church, independent
of synod or council. Talk of the Pope's supremacy after that. For
the articles as modified &c. in the reign of Elizabeth, see pp. 582,
583; and regarding the state of parties in the church and their
differences, Burnet says, (p. 584) that "*if the animosities and heats
that are raised by them are well examined, there is scarce any probable
hopes left of composing those differences, unless our lawgivers do
vigorously apply themselves to it.*"

(62) I have alluded in the preface to O'Connell's remark on the
tolerating spirit of the Irish Catholics. During Mary's persecution
of the Protestants in England "*the Catholic corporation of Dublin
opened 74 houses in Dublin, at their own expense, to receive and
shelter the Protestants who sought refuge in Ireland from the fury of
the English government.*" (O'Neill Daunt's catechism of the History
of Ireland, p. 59). The alleged massacre of Protestants in 1641 has
been amply disproved by the discrepancies of their own writers;
some of whom give down the number killed at even twice or thrice the
amount of the whole Protestant population at the time. Lord

When England then through reformation went,
What was the issue of that great event?
When from the Papal sovereignty freed,
How did religion in the land succeed?
How far were morals with the creed restored,
When Henry reigned as its superior lord?
Did gladdened virtue wider ope her wings,
When Christian faith became the sport of kings?
Let history answer,—and the stern reply
Will not indeed the improvement testify.
When cursed Popery's dominion fled
Blessed licentiousness walked in instead;
And pious rapine made reform agree
To change of faith that changed men's property.
The rich church lands and abbeys' broad domains
Were of right doctrine the substantial gains;

Clarendon, who states that 40,000 or 50,000 Protestants lost their lives, admits that " *About the beginning of November, the English and Scotch forces in Carrickfergus, murdered, in one night, all the inhabitants of the Island Gee (commonly called Mac Gee) to the number of 3000 men, women and children, all innocent persons, in a time when none of the Catholics of that country were in arms or rebellion. Note that this was the first massacre committed in Ireland on either side.*" (Clar. Hist. Rev. p. 329, cited by Plowden in his history, vol i. p. 137, note.) Clarendon also tells us that *the English garrisons commenced burning, pillaging and murdering in Munster, before any rebellion began there* (Ibid. p. 396; and Plowden Ib.) But if "*the first massacre*" was committed on the English Protestant side in November, how, as Plowden remarks, can the great massacre by the Catholics on the 23rd. October be substantiated? The fact seems to be this—that the "*extirpation*" of the Irish Catholics was resolved upon, as Clarendon proves (p. 215) and Warner (Hist. of the Reb. p. 176) and Carte (Life of Ormond, vol. i, p. 330) and Leland (Hist. of Ireland, Book v. chap 4) and the English Protestants, settlers and soldiers, suffering severely in the attempt to effect it, the myth of the massacre was invented, at once to avenge and account for their losses.

And for the sake of truth reform endows
Hypocrisy and fraud, and broken vows.
As the new gospel freedom is attained,
Old bridled passions are no more restrained;
And lusty churchmen tire of rigorous lives,
While their great chief replaces murdered wives.*

How blest the church of Henry's bold abscission
Whose head assumes no clerical position!
'Tis no transmission from the Holy Ghost
That qualifies for the most sacred post.
Who rules the nation also rules the creed,
Not *chosen*, but *entitled* to succeed,
Nor ordination needs in his behalf,
If proved a Tudor, Stuart, or a Guelph.
Than this, perhaps, we see no greater change
That from the ancient did the new estrange :—
One that can truly fill no hierarch's see
Even the highest of the Church must be
In this inscrutable theology.

With us the Pope, being Pope, is sovereign too ;
But being Sovereign makes the Pope with you.
"Henry taught right :"—if so, the Apostles erred
When Herod for their head was not preferred.
Herod and *Henry* well together sound,
And semblant actions make them both renowned.
The main catastrophe of Herod's reign
Pass by: still is the mutual likeness plain.
When one his living kinsman's wife had wed,
John blamed the adultery and lost his head ;
And Henry's wrath pursued the Pope, when he
Refused to sanction *his* adultery.

* See additional note A.

But then you say "all this is understood,
The means were evil; yet the work is good."
'Tis true the mystic ways of Providence
Are far beyond the reach of mortal sense.
God does not always His best loved depute
His sovereign will on earth to execute.
Thus were the gentile's victories decreed,
That Israel from bondage might be freed;
And thus, though Cyrus would to Jove incline,
It was Jehovah's thunder gave the sign.
Oft rage ungodly, too, by God was sent
For His unfaithful people's punishment.
Rage punished guilt with an appointed sword
But never yet revealed God's peaceful Word,
And in Reform a novel mission hath,
To settle simply what is *Christian faith.*

Yet these are difficulties that must strike
Reformers in their progress all alike;
But in your special way some others fall,
That make it seem the most ill-starred of all.
Those are apparent where your creed protects
Plain Romish points denounced by other sects,
Who, from old Roman faith more segregate,
At least are more consistent in their hate;
But over *your* mere mongrel scheme impends,
With our dislike, the censure of your friends.
Those specks of Catholicity you prize
But make you more unlovely in our eyes—
Even as the landscape, dreary under snow,
Looks drearier where the green begins to show;
And by each party more from us retired
Even less than Catholics you seem admired:

They find your link between us and their sects
Less worth than the extreme objects it connects.
   Yet all " Reformers' " plans are so devised,
That each is by his brethren scandalized ;
Who, trampling the old faith beneath their feet,
Produce but tumult, contest and deceit.
To this, the warning mercy hath designed,
Some, in their hate of Rome, are wholly blind.
The Reformation still to them appears
Unblamable and stirs no doubts or fears :
Wide radiating in a murky sky,
Its beams impose upon the thoughtless eye,
Like the bright columns, that, in wintry days,
Divergent, often pass for solar rays,
As from behind thick clouds they seem to run,
And are but mists around a darkened sun.
   We now, in fine, have variously tried
The faith reformed and are not edified.
We seek its excellence in sundry ways,
Yet nothing of it find that's meet for praise :
Neither the manner of its rise, nor those
Infuriate people, from whose rage it rose ;
Nor, in its system, can we more esteem,
Even for ingenuity, the scheme.
Let the inquirer search and scrutinize
As his most patient wit can best devise,
By every method seek its meaning well,
By every supposition possible,
Trying, when, in one view, it is not plain,
If, in another, it may brightness gain ;
But, when he thus would make the sense more clear,
It, ten to one, will wholly disappear.

Yes! Let the Reformation thus be tried,
Investigated closely on each side,
And who investigates can only see
Defects, where all is not obscurity,
Even to the present from its earliest dates.—
Confusion sprung it and perpetuates.

No blest perfection can we then behold,
In any view, to win us to your fold:
Further, if works count not, but faith—a tenet
That you maintain, and your works show you
    mean it—[63]
Then it is only by the want of faith
We can run risk of spiritual death;
And Catholics are surely free from such,
Who only, at the worst, believe *too much.*
Still if you say the Church of England gives
The choicest food on which the spirit lives:
If thus her doctrines the best faith disclose—
And what they are precisely, the Lord knows!—[64]

(63) Yet Anglicans are not so opposed to the Catholic doctrine of good works and rewards as they themselves seem to imagine. They will argue to the last against it; and still they say the following *Collect*, called by them the "*stir up*," on every twenty-fifth Sunday after Trinity: "*Stir up, we beseech thee, O Lord, the wills of thy faithful people; that they plenteously bringing forth the fruit of good works, may of thee be plenteously rewarded, through Jesus Christ our Lord.*"

(64) What constitutes an Anglican, further than a civil connection with the Establishment, it would be vain to enquire. As for the test of the Thirty-nine articles, no one would think of applying it at the present day; and even at earlier periods, we find that they were not excluded from the decisions of private judgment. Gibbon says [Decline and Fall. conclusion of c. liv.] "since the days of Luther and Calvin, a secret reformation has been silently working in the bosom of the reformed churches....The doctrine of a protestant

No matter—if you *think* them strictly right,
And must indulge your wish to proselyte,
Your Christian teaching should at least not stray,
For vile incentives, from a Christian way,
Nor prove in Heaven's cause what poets tell
In heathen lore—that zeal was born of hell.
And still your proselyting zeal might fix
On others better than us Catholics,
Who possess *faith*, and, even in such store,
'Tis *less* would make us Protestants—*not more.*

church is far removed from the knowledge or belief of its private members, and the forms of orthodoxy, the articles of faith, are subscribed with a sigh or a smile by the modern clergy. Yet the friends of Christianity are alarmed at the boundless impulse of inquiry and scepticism. The predictions of the Catholics are accomplished &c."

Gibbon cannot be suspected of much favoritism toward Catholics; but still he may not be considered a sufficient authority in matters relating to Anglicanism, and therefore, in the following extract, I add the indisputable testimony of Burnet:—"I have always had a true zeal for the Church of England; I have lived in its communion with great joy, and have pursued its true interests with an unfeigned affection : yet I must say there are many things in it, that have been very uneasy to me.

" *The requiring subscriptions to the Thirty-nine articles is a great imposition.* I believe them all myself; but as those about original sin and predestination might be expressed more unexceptionably, so I think it a better way to let such matters continue to be still the standard of doctrine, with some few corrections, and to censure those who teach any contrary tenets, than to oblige all that serve in the church to subscribe them. *The greater part subscribe without ever examining them ; and others do it because they must do it* though they can hardly satisfy their consciences about some things in them." [Burnet's Hist. of his own Times, Fol. Ed. vol. ii. pp. 379, 380.] At the present day we find a very general demand in the Establishment for a reformation of the articles. Paley, in his defence of the Feathers' Tavern petitioners in 1772, states it as an admitted fact that the only persons who then believed the Articles were the Methodists, who were refused ordination by the Bishops. [Edinburgh Review, 1853, note to page 275.]

250 clergymen presented this Feathers' Tavern Petition to Parliament. Its prayer was that the Petitioners might be relieved from subscription to the 39 articles and 'restored to their rights, as Protestants, of interpreting scripture for themselves, without being bound by any human explications thereof.' Paley, in the pamphlet which he published in defence of these Petitioners, acknowledges that they 'continue in the Church without being able to reconcile to their belief every proposition imposed upon them by subscription; and speaks of them as ' impatient under the yoke.' (Paley's collected works, p. 362.)

The Edinburgh Review, from which I have taken the foregoing, concludes a very able exposition of " *Church Parties*" in England as follows:—" While civil discord thus convulses the Church, many of her children are falling away from her, and abandoning the distinctive doctrines of Christianity. We have already noticed the diffusion of infidel opinions among the lower classes; but the mischief is not confined to them. The highest ranks and most intelligent professions are influenced by sceptical opinions, to an extent which, twenty years back, would have seemed incredible. This state of things, as far as the upper classes are concerned, has been directly caused by the dissensions of the Church. ' When Doctors differ who shall decide' is the expression of an almost inevitable scepticism. These unnatural hostilities must cease, if we are ever to reconvert the Pagans of the factory, or the Pantheists of the forum." The Reviewer would have peace established between the various parties, and recommends the rather difficult decision to acknowledge " a substantial unity of faith, and an absolute identity of holiness in the midst of endless diversity of opinion," and " to turn to the true battle which is raging round us ; a battle not between Anglicans and Calvinists, nor even between Popery and Protestantism, but between Faith and infidelity." (Edinburgh Review, 1853, pp. 341, 342.)

ANGLICANIA.

—

PART IV.

PART IV.

Then, Anglicans, leave us with faith alone
But teach its blessings where they are not known.
Apply, at home, your spiritual cure
To learned atheist and creedless boor,— *
Or yet to those who, mocking Heaven, reveal
The sombre sabbath-test of faith genteel,—
At home, in gold-adoring England, where
Unscrupulousness makes the millionaire,—
Where fraud is sure to win the highest prize,
And honesty scarce fails to pauperize.
　　Consider well how England's treasures stored
Oft point to faith and charity ignored.—
Perhaps the fortune of this wealthy knave
Was made by forging fetters for the slave;
Or manufactured Pagan gods may be
A proof of his profane cupidity.
Yet, while in wealth the Englishman excels,
Unequalled wretchedness in England dwells;
And while gilt bibles and fine pews abound,
More extreme vices nowhere else are found.
The wealth of England spurs the sin of pride;
And to sin, too, is her distress allied.
For here the fleshly forces so control,
That a starved body makes a perished soul.

* See additional note B.

Here boundless luxury and pomp abide,
And hungry squalor shivers at their side :
All the enjoyments money can command,
And moaning misery on the other hand.
Repulsive manners all around we see—
Rude lofty rank, and rude vulgarity.[65]
And yet not seldom we may surely find
In every station here a polished mind.
Real refinement oft in England glows,
And highest intellect she ever shows,
But low-raised natures on all sides oppose.

Here too are the full beauties of man's shape,
And human forms scarce raised above the ape ;
For where the parent the child's mind besots,
Where evil flourishes and virtue rots,
Diseases foul become a certain fate, .
And bent deformity perpetuate.
The poisoned blood long coursing through the veins
From sire to son transmits degenerate stains,

(65) I do not give this character of the English from my own
observations. It is admitted by themselves; for instance, in Doctor
Shaw's "Travels in England," 1861, he complains that—" our manners, which ought to have been refined, courteous and condescending,
are bluff, blunt, inconsiderate, unsympathising, rude and selfish
among every class of the community ;" (p. 307) and the habits and
manners of the working people are " of such a nature, and their
intellectual condition so low as to render them interesting objects of
study." (p. 268.) He observes that "the ignorance of our people is
such, and that not confined to the working classes, as places them
below the people of Scotland, infinitely below the same classes in
all our dependencies, and vastly inferior to many of the continental
kingdoms." (p. 307.) For some of the tricks of trade by which
fortunes are amassed, the recognized impossibility of honestly
acquiring them, the manufacture of false jewels, Pagan gods and
manacles for the Indians and Negroes, &c. see "Travels in England,"
chap. xxviii.

And the impure inheritance we find
In the shrunk body and imbruted mind.[66]
    Little the hate of Popery avails
Where so the entire social system fails.
And what absurdity would dare demand
For England still the name of "Happy Land?"
If some, beyond belief, their coffers fill,
Who, thence, can say the land is happy still?
The *"people"* are not happy, and by those
It is that countries their true state disclose.

(66) Neither are my remarks, which apply to the low moral and physical state of the working classes in England, derived from any impressions of my own, but from the statements of the best observers in the country itself. The *Times* (Aug. 5, 1858) exclaimed against England's improving her breed of horses, &c. and allowing her "breed of men to fall into hopeless degeneracy." Doctor Shaw, commenting on the above, quotes from *Horne's Report* the "abundant evidences of the degenerating of the working classes—'the chief diseases to which they are subject are curvature and distortion of the spine, deformity of the limbs, malformation of the pelvis, &c. ;'" and we are told that out of 613 men enlisted in six different places only 238 were approved for service; and in Nottingham, Derby, and Leicester, which are not worse than a score of other places, it is next to impossible for any one among thousands of afflicted females to be the mother of a healthy babe. ("Travels in England," page 373) At an Industrial School visited by Dr. Shaw, "among many hundreds of children, seated on their forms, scarcely a healthy, good-looking child could be found ...The low standard of morality that belonged to the parents sat upon the countenances of these children in all its hideousness and deformity....The poor little creatures had been poisoned with the bad blood of immoral and corrupt parents for many generations." (pp. 211, 212.) "In no part of the world are the classes so much apart as in England;" and, contrasting the extremely rich and the extremely poor, Dr. Shaw describes the latter as "diminutive, stiff in the joints, sickly and pale faced, ragged in costume, rough in manners, and resembling a race of aboriginal savages, rather than the well-grown people of England, such as may be seen in Rotten Row during the London Season." (p. 269.)

Only a race as happy can be prized
As they in happiness are equalized :
Not happy by the o'ergrown wealth of classes,
But the sufficient comforts of the masses.
What cares the English pauper to be told,
No land like his can boast such stores of gold?
What care those wretches coiled in filthy styes,
That daylight on the empire never dies?[67]
What care they to be told of England's reign—
Dreadful on land and matchless on the main?

(67) The following observations of Dr. Shaw apply, not to any manufacturing locality, not to a town "infested with low Irish," as the phrase goes, but to that very fashionable watering-place, Brighton.

After describing some most revolting individual cases of moral, intellectual and physical debasement, Dr. Shaw tells us that he was " occupied for several hours in visiting these wretched dens, which abound in this district, where the accumulation of filth on the walls seemed to be as old as the foundation of the building, the aspect of which chills the blood and turns the stomach. In some of these abodes the light of heaven scarcely enters to illuminate the dismal scene....The odour is deathlike; it seems as if it came from the charnel house." (" Travels in England," pp. 157, 158.)

A writer in the *London Review*, showing that " the miserable condition of the bulk of the labouring people" is not confined to large towns and cities, describes their state in the small community of Bridport as illustrative of that fact. He exclaims :—" It is easy for the self-complacent Englishman to praise the British people and nation," and concludes an account enough to satiate the most depraved appetite for the abominable, by asking those, who subscribe large funds for the conversion of savages, whether their charity might not be better applied at home. At the same time he observes the difficulty "for morality and religion to make way among a population that live in habitual filth of person......That know as little of the decencies of life as the brutes that perish....huddled together in human pigstyes." (See *L. Review* of July 20, 1861.) Bridport is in Dorsetshire, and free from the " *nasty Irish*" element.

What boots it them to know a threatening hour
Can only prove the greatness of her power?
Nor will hope curl to smiles those quivering lips
By mock-battalions and half-armored ships.
    Of energetic action England boasts:
But ask true Christian feeling *what it costs.*
See if the labor, which she calls her pride,
Lays not humanity and faith aside.
She labors truly; yet the boast is vain,
Which brings her joy, but more amount of pain:
For here though rapine and the luck of trade
Earth's proudest aristocracy have made,
The real laborers, the luckless poor,
A worse than negro slavery endure;
And they who *work,* but wage an endless strife
With suffering, for mere support of life.
See the deep mine, whose ceaseless shadows roll,
As on the eyes, the same upon the soul!
Behold the grimy savage here upgrown!
To him remain man's joys and hopes unknown:
To him the cheering voice of Faith is mute—
His aspirations shared in by the brute.
Down in the earth immured, where nature's light
Disturbs not deep, eternal, hideous night,
And deadly airs explosive ever play
Around the guarded taper's dismal ray—
Here, death-encompassed, 'mid the twinkling
        gloom,
The wretch unpitied bears his hopeless doom.
That which he seeks brings not to him its gains,
Nor tells him the great secrets it contains.

From earth's own scriptures, though he turns the
    leaves,
No 'teaching of God's glory he receives.
What in this charry mass can him amaze,
Or prove a motive toward his maker's praise?
He sees in it no traces of Divine
Wonders of power, mysteries of design :—
He knows not that he works among the tombs
Of ancient worlds, that the new earth inhumes ;
Nor dreams that, once, those treasures of the abyss
Lived for the sunbeam and night's dewy kiss,
Where giant-reeds and towering ferns, on high,
Crested the earth beneath an ancient sky.

  Yet while those truths must piety inspire,
Faith does not still their wondrous aid require.
The miner well might earn his daily bread,
Though with this knowledge troubling not his head,
And still by Christian faithfulness be led.
But in your Bible-land it is not so ;
For faith the grim barbarian does not know :
Unknown the wonders the Creator wrought ;
Nor of his mercies has the wretch been taught ;
But England's wealth is by his arms supplied ;
And England's piety is satisfied.[68]

  (68) The wretched state of ignorance in which the *great proportion*
of the English mining population is plunged has become too notorious to require proofs. The miner who, on being asked who Jesus
Christ was, replied that *he did not know him, but that, perhaps, he*
worked in the next pit, may be taken as a type of his class ; though
I question if his religious ideas are much below those of his brother
boors of the upper world, who might bless the maker of the green
fields and the blue skies. The *Quarterly Review* says of the Welsh
Miners, " Ill trained by parent, *seldom warned by priest*, yet enjoying
wages which place sensual gratification within reach of an unspiritual-

See now the cursed *factory* consume
Infancy's tenderness and youth's full bloom!
Where tortures, that both soul and body kill,
Are offered up to wealth's great demon still.
Here the same coal, that in deep earth was found,
Now sends the wheel in its perpetual round;
And, mingled with the smoke that blots the skies,
The ceaseless moans of laboring weakness rise.
On, ever on: still at the work unblest;
Nor eve nor midnight brings the sufferer rest;
Or if exhausted sleepy nature droops,
Even perhaps to death the victim stoops.
Well might the demon the rich product boast,
If valued by the suffering it cost:
For not earth's brightest gems could fairly buy
What draws from innocence one single sigh.
But when did wrongs or pains of others find
Consideration in the hoarder's mind?
It little matters to the *cotton lord*
How others wept while he his riches stored.
He little heeds the fainting laberer's cry;
And, though the colored web his slaves supply—
Perhaps in some far tropic land to pall
The dusky shoulders of the cannibal—
Had caught the tears that English childhood rained,
Or with the blood of tender hands was stained,
Yet seems his conscience not the less content;
And in his piety full confident

ized nature, these men are found precisely in that state most
calculated to break down the moral being and to throw back
humanity into barbarism." (vol. lxxxv. p. 337.)

He yet may be, amid his hoarded heaps : —*
He hates the Pope—and *awful Sabbaths keeps !*
  Thus England's worship of her God behold,
And of her super-Deity of gold !
While the poor Celt is called on to revere
The energy of Saxon character;
To praise the industry the Saxon shows;
While gains accursed its boasted fruits disclose.
But in the Christian bosom of the Celt
The long-sought reverence is still unfelt.
The energy you boast as England's fame
Seems to the Christian but reproach and shame.
Better as poorest of the earth to pine,
Than as the richest by its means to shine :—·
If by it only we can prosperous be,
God still preserve us from prosperity !
  Yes : go to England whom you so revere,
And see how far her faith is now sincere.
To judge her virtue, well investigate
The contradictions in her social state.
Where some so feeble are and some so strong,
With such extremes there's plainly something
    wrong—
Some rottenness upon the system's face
Which took the Reformation as its base—
A base upon pretended freedom fixed,
With politics and doctrine intermixed;
And if this system did true faith attest,
Sad were the consequence of being blest.
  But England is not blest : her social ties
Are too wide severed ; and her doctrine dies.
     * See additional note C.

Splitting in sects and sects, at length we see
Its final phase is infidelity :
Like some great ice-field in the increasing day,
It first breaks up, and then melts quite away.
Ireland's misfortunes that from *others* came
Have fixed no blot upon her moral fame :
But not so England's : her misfortune's cause
Exists *within herself* and her own laws :—
From her own sins the woes of England come ;
And Ireland's sufferings are martyrdom.
Who doubts that misery in England springs
From an imperfect moral state of things ?
And better then to her your care extend,
Than your fine zeal on Irish faith to spend.
Go then to her ; and labor to efface
Each social ill and irreligious trace ;
Or at least try her people's woful fate
From downright unbelief to separate.
Yet if in vain your pious aid we ask
For this untempting and too hopeless task, [69]
Then bring your doctrine to each distant race
That anti-christian principles debase.
For this go nobly forth to distant lands.
Seek the dread climes where Africa expands ;
Where human victims to the Fetish fall
By pestilential Zaire or Senegal.
Go where the icy Himalayas rise
To the high winter of the torrid skies ;

(69) Dr. Shaw was informed that the clergyman of a district in
Brighton appointed a missionary ; but the man finding his work too
hard and too hazardous, relinquished his post. ("Travels in England," p. 159.) This is worthy of remark in various points of view.

Set in whose azure, sunlit summits gleam
Above the worshipped Ganges' infant stream ;
And the white vastness of mount Everest
Supreme looks far o'er heathen realms unblest ;
While scarce less great Dhawalagiri glows,
Offering back to heaven his virgin snows,
Beloved by Brahmins in his glittering pride,
With Vishnu's stony symbols on his side.[70]
Visit the scenes where Annam's temples stand ;
Or where grim idols curse "The Flowery Land."—
Advance along Manchuria's pagan shore,—
Old Asia's far secluded tracts explore :
Where wretched souls dire superstition fills,
From Pechelee, across "The Silver Hills,"
To the low Caspian:—midst the blossomed plains,
Where the wild rose impedes the wandering trains,
And tulips bend beneath the Tartars' cars :—
By "sacred" Lasa to "The Sea of Stars :"—
Through Aksu, brightly clad with cotton flowers ;
And where the Thian Shan o'er Shamo towers.
Or, going by Altaian passes forth,
Traverse the rude and unconverted north.
By Lena's shore the frozen Tundra cross,
Drawn by the deer that nips the scanty moss ;
Even to Siberia's ice-armored coast,
Where the big mammoths lie embalmed in frost.
Or, when the Arctic sea's freed surges roll,
And midnight suns shine from below the Pole,

(70) The Salagrana Ammonites, esteemed by the Brahmins as
symbolical of the testaceous incarnation of Vishnu. (*Humboldt's
Ansichten der natur.*)

Confront the priest, who savage breasts excites
By Shaman orgies and unholy rites.
In Syrian deserts seek the Arab's tent;
And preach beneath the glowing firmament,
By the wrecked temple of Palmyra's god,
Where sculptured shafts o'er desolation nod;
And porphyry pillars, hewn by skilful hands,
Lie with their shadows 'mid the drifting sands:
Here teach him, who in prayer toward Mecca turns,
To venerate the Gospel he now spurns.
Or far beyond the wide Atlantic speed;
And through Columbia's wastes extend the creed.
Instruct the Indian hunter roaming o'er
The moose-deer haunts of Athabasca's shore.
Convert the Puri of Brazilian woods,
And Trumpet-worshipper by Tomo's floods.
The bulky Patagonian address;
Or find the utmost island-wilderness,
When fuchsias cheer the dreary landscape's frown;
And, when the Southern Cross looks nightly down
On the poor savage by Magellan's waves,
Point to the starry sign; and tell of Him who saves.
'Tis thus, indeed, that you might justly claim
The honest missionary's honored fame;
And, even though erring, show your pure intent
Was still the Gospel's wide establishment;
Moving the softened savage to adore
The God of whom he never heard before;
And making barbarous nations fondly prize
The name of Christian that they now despise.
Thus you might cause the faithful to revere
A work in faithless lands at least sincere;

And stand as *Christian rivals* of that Rome,
You strive with now, as *Christian foes* at home :
Your zeal not worldly, in a false attire,
But like that given by the Tongues of Fire.
　We yet deny not that the Protestant
May often Christianity implant
In heathen lands, and, while we censure you,
To men like him we give the honor due.
Oh, that we might his mission's spirit call
The zeal of British doctrine national !
But different the zeal that rather leads
To cloak with sanctity its cruel deeds
Where the soon-conquered weak barbarian
　　bleeds.
Thus we have seen "HUMILIATION-DAY,"
When Anglicans agreed to *fast and pray.*
And what was the ephemeral rigor's cause ?—
Was it obedience to sacred laws ?
Or was it sorrow for their former crimes,
While vowing justice during future times—
Sorrow for outrage and oppression dire,
That raised in Indian breasts the vengeful fire—
For all the acts that maddened injured men :—
Was this "HUMILIATION'S" motive then ?
No sure : not thus to penance were they brought !
Thus they would bargain for some object sought !
What then was the most grave and righteous
　　thing
They would so purchase from the Eternal King ?
Success in slaughter and each vengeful deed !
For that the MISSION's Church would intercede !

Sackcloth and ashes must for that be tried,
And one day's gluttony be left aside!
Is this the teaching of the God that died? [71]
　You wage, indeed, a wild eccentric war
'Gainst our humiliations regular:
For, though you've fasts well fixed, the same as we,
And for the same intent, in theory,
You blame the fasts we practise to control
Unholy impulses and help the soul,
Only at periods favoring the use
Of fasting when fierce passions are let loose;
Your object, not those passions to restrain,
But to move God your fury to sustain;
So, while we fast to make our sinning less,
You, when you fast, would not your sin repress,
But bribe high Heaven for your sin's success.
　The daring paths that Southern genius traced
Over the ocean's old mysterious waste
England pursued, with plunder for her aim,
Where glorious exploits gave to others fame.

(71) We all remember the day of "*humiliation and prayer*," by which England, on the occasion of the great Sepoy revolt, prepared for acts like those which will be found described in a note at the end. We remember, too, how the spirit of blood was evoked at the time by the English Press and in the pulpit. An extract from a *sermon* addressed by the most popular preacher of the day to an audience of 26,000 *humiliation*-performers will serve to show the sentiments with which a people sought to propitiate the God of mercy—The Revd. preacher said—" he looked upon the gallows as a frightful evil; he regarded every gibbet as a dreadful visitation on the land; but these (meaning the Indians) were rebels *to be executed; they must be punished*, for both *Heaven* and earth demanded it."

8

When toward the "Cape of Storms" the Portuguese
Shaped his adventurous course through unknown
    seas,
And nightly watched to see the *star-clouds* roll
Around the darkly rising southern pole,
He thought not that he piloted the way
Of ruin then to India or Cathay.
But we have witnessed in succeeding times
The deeds of England in those teeming climes.
In China, where our martyrs preached the truth,
She trafficked poison at the cannon's mouth;
And in that India, where at first she came
A timid trader, we have seen her fame
Extended in relentless conquest o'er
The shrieking land.   From long subdued Mysore
Even to outraged Oude we saw it spread:
Nor, from old Comorin's sun-beaten head
To where the Macedonian king recoiled,
Remains a spot of India undespoiled.

   Her dread unsparing system we have viewed,
Grinding a feeble race in servitude;
By active warfare, or force-threatening frauds
Annexing kingdoms while her Church applauds,—
Humiliating that she may maintain
The old aggressive vigor of her reign:
For scruples territorial we miss
When *India* reads for *Savoy* or for *Nice*.

   Yes! we know well the long continued base
Inflictions on the wretched Indian race;
And we have seen how rage barbaric leads
Retaliation to ferocious deeds;

While re-requitals, more ferocious still,
Would seem your gospel ordinance to fulfil.
  The plundering victors tortured, slew and burned,
Till India on the heel that trod her turned.[72]
They then from heaven would retribution wring,
As even made martyrs by their victim's sting,
And for the new blood-struggle well prepare
By deep "Humiliation's" fast and prayer.
Success ensues; nor must we dare to scan
God's purpose in the acts of man with man.
That Heaven oft permits the stronger race, .
Against Heaven's laws, the weaker to oppress,
Is plain to all; but why it should be so
We must remain contented not to know.
Why sin exists is far beyond our ken:
Sin against God, ourselves, and other men.
But this we know; succeeding in the offence
Is not of impious prayer the consequence.
'Twas not the heathen's sacrifice availed
When he, victorious, God's own tribes assailed;
And shall we say her *day of humbling* gave
England's new force to immolate the slave ?
  The shootings, stranglings, from the cannon
     blown,
Into slow fires the living wretches thrown ;*
Confiding youths, heirs of a native crown,
Urged to submit, then faithlessly shot down;
Pillage and waste and outrages untold ;
And all for lust of empire, lust of gold :

(72) The mode of levying taxes by *torture* in India was exposed
long since.
        * See additional note D.

Are these the acts on which the righteousness
Of England humbling would invoke success?
Is it for this she makes her grave appeal,
And to the God of Christians dares to kneel?
  How often great success beneath the skies
In want of mercy and fine feeling lies!
When virtuous sensibilities impede,
In things sublunary few men succeed.
The obdurate may easily attain
What is impossible to the humane.
Humanity dilutes our selfish force,
And leaves us losers in the worldly course.
And still the unfeeling man we often find
Praised in success for virtuous traits of mind:
For many their ideal of virtue draw
From the oft wrongful code of civil *law*;
Not from the heart, nor have the virtuous sense
To see when laws make rights that conscience calls
      pretence.
  As single tempers, so are nations' hearts:
The whole is like its homogeneous parts;
And in those lands where sense of right most fails,
Aptness for wealth and conquest most prevails.
Yet better, possibly, we might refer
To other causes this worst character.—
Nations may be unjust as they are strong,
Not differing in tendency to wrong:
For, though there are just men, the aggregate
Is, certainly, not just in any state;
And power proves the ancient Scripture truth:—
Man's heart is prone to evil from his youth.[73]

(73) Gen. viii. 21.

Not better, then, than other lands, nor worse
May England be in her destroying course.[74]
'Tis so, perhaps ; but while her rule depends
On force, to extra virtue she pretends.
This fault at least is specially her own.—
Let tribes and nations still beneath her groan:
Let not one evil passion be restrained
By which her wealth or conquests may be gained :
Let Him who Peter told to sheathe his sword
Be, when it suits, forgotten or ignored ;
But then admit that fact ; nor still lay claim
To special veneration for His name ;
For vice that boasts not must as virtue shine,
Compared with vice which styles itself divine.

    While England spreads abroad her conquering
        fame,
Where feeble races tremble at her name,
Rome conquers too, but conquers with the light
Of faith dispelling unbelief's long night.
In British land her missions are unknown,
Save those that guard the piety of *her own.*
But in strange climes the Saviour's light extends
From Rome indeed. Hers is the saint who bends
His weary steps to pull the idol down,
Or in Christ's service gain a martyr's crown.[75]

(74) This opinion, however, is not shared in by the author of " my
Diary in India," who maintains that " there is no such enemy to a
black skin as your Anglo-Saxon who has done so much for liberty."
(vol. i, p. 190.)

(75) The great suffering and great success of Catholic missionaries,
compared with any others, has been often proved. The success of
Protestant missions to the Heathen is not considerable. See Mr.
Marshall's late work—" Christian Missions ; their Agents, their
Method and their Results."

Distress and fortitude, in every age,
Of Christ's true followers are the heritage;
And, wandering with desert-dusted feet,
Their *purses* not with *rent-charge* spoil replete,[76]
Without the zeal of pious fools to thank
For, every day, fresh "orders on the bank,"
Through the dark regions of the earth they rove
And teach the revelation of God's love.
No man by them offended, none defamed—
So that their ministry may not be blamed—
In all their teaching to the soul that errs
They show themselves as *God's true ministers.*
Patient in dire necessities, nor less
Patient *in stripes* and *manacled distress,*
In *watchings, fastings, chastity,* they prove
The Spirit's guidance. Charitable love,
Sweetness and truth are still their mission's signs;
And where they walk *bright-armor'd justice*
        shines,—[77]
Poor in the things of earth, but in the store
Of Heaven so *rich* that they want nothing more.[78]
So labors, then, the Catholic, while you
Your comfortable MISSION here pursue.
In reverend ease, well-guarded, and well-paid,
You ply your doctrine's profitable trade,
With well-filled purses and fair ladies' smiles
To stimulate your missionary wiles,
And the shrill shouts of Papist children rude
To measure your extent of fortitude.

        (76) Mark vi. 8.   (77) 2 Cor. vi. 3—7.
                (78) Ibid. ver. 10.

Nor *fasts* nor *watchings* prove that heavenly springs
Supply your zeal midst fleshly sufferings.
Instead of *patience* and of *truth*, you prize
Rage everlasting and defaming lies.
Oppressive actions on your serfs we see
Taking the place of Christian charity.
You show your *sweetness* when you preach upon
" The idolatries and crimes of Babylon,"
And then to *justice* you thus prove your claim—
You rob that "Babylon" which you defame.[79]

(79) The denunciations of Rome by our Anglican missionaries
may be illustrated by an example taken from an invitation to attend
one of their meetings, concluding with the usual phrase—"Roman
Catholics bring your Bibles, come and hear," and published in the
Irish Times of Sept. 12, 1862. The quality of the religion that must
be ascribed to the authors of this invitation may be inferred from a
perverted text, a garbled text, and a text used as an unchristian
insult, all of which it contains in a small space, and which I give in
the following extract:—" Subject for discussion—is the Church of
Rome the Church of Christ?—' For the mystery of iniquity *already*
worketh.' 2 Thess. ii. 7, Dr. Cullen's R. C. Bible.—There are 126
sentences of anathema in the Council of Trent, though St. Paul wrote
to the Church of Rome ' Bless and curse not.' Romans xii. 14.—
'And on her forehead (the woman's—the apostate Church—verse 3)
a name was written : A mystery ; Babylon the great, the mother of
the fornications (i. e. idolatries) and the abominations of the earth.'
Apoc. xvii. 5, Dr. Cullen's approved edition of the Roman Catholic
Scriptures." In this precious production we find a text, which was
obviously applied by St. Paul to the contemporary commencement of
heresy, such as appeared in Cerinthus, plainly perverted in its meaning : for here it is applied to the *Church itself*, which would thus be
shown to have required the reforming services of a Luther even in
the time of the Apostles. The various and wonderful absurdities
that are suggested by this *missionary* interpretation must be apparent
to any ordinary intellect.

By the garbling of another text the meaning of the sacred writer
is concealed ; and the suppression of a part would make an injunc-
tion to brotherly love and charity appear as a command to the
Church not to exercise a power decreed to her elsewhere ; while her

With boundless appetite your MISSION feeds
On social strife and scatters discord's seeds.
Where Protestants and Catholics would cease
Their ancient contests it forbids the peace.
Through countries, districts, provinces, elate
With evil power, it engenders hate.
Where different faiths prevail, it even tries
To break the sacredness of kindred ties,
And, poised on leathern wing, delights to move
Amid the ruins of domestic love.
As most propitious to its cause it hails
The time when, famine-struck, a nation wails.
The breath of woe it gladly scents from far ;
And pestilence becomes its guiding star.

pronouncing of anathemas would be proved unscriptural even by
persons who say "*Amen*" to the *curses* of the "*Commination Service*"
as appointed by the *Book of Common Prayer!* The unchristian
insult to Catholics conveyed in the use of the third text needs no
comment.

Thus is the Holy Scripture handled by its pretended chief reverers,
and thus it is interpreted by those who would have it studied "without note or comment." But with all their solicitude for our papistical souls the less spiritual objects of Anglican missionary ardor are
never forgotten by those religious *artistes ;* and that our missionaries
keep at least one eye always open to *business,* may be perceived by an
advertisement immediately preceding the one in question. The
former document, which probably got the place of honor on the
principle that the substance is more worthy than the shadow, contains an "URGENT APPEAL" for assistance toward a treasury approaching exhaustion. Its replenishment is demanded on the grounds that
the conversions effected by its means—"one and another, month
after month"—were wondrous ; and still more extraordinary were
its services in "*strengthening the minds* of Roman Catholics to resist
the false authority of the priesthood." The writers conclude in a
strain of pious confidence, predicting the sure appearance of the
solicited cash while "praying in faith with the Psalmist—'establish
thou the *work* of our hands *upon us,* &c.' "

'Tis then, indeed, it glows with brightest hope,
And, tempting misery, its coffers ope.
Then each soul-killing prize is best displayed.
But why, O Heaven, permit the cursed trade?
Yet can we wonder, when the demon showed
His gifts, permitted even to tempt his God?

Your MISSION still, in less unprosperous years,
Spies out each place where misery appears,
Into the death-pale ear its poison pours
Among our mountains and remote sea-shores:
Or if you find not wretchedness, your plan
Is by all means *to make it* where you can;
And so you wield, to prove your Bible true,
Not it alone, but now your *crowbar* too.
And is it in Christ's name that crowbar fills
With desolation Partry's vales and hills?
Is it in Christ's blest name the cottage falls,
And happy homes are turned to shattered walls?[80]

(80) Who has not heard of the *Partry* evictions by Lord Plunket,
Protestant Bishop of Tuam? I will give a few extracts from a long
article that appeared on this subject in *The Sun* newspaper of Jan.
5, 1861. Speaking of the ejectment cases tried at Ballinrobe
sessions, The Sun says :—

"On two points the evidence is as clear as it could well be—that
the Bishop, through his agent, required his tenants-at-will to send
their children to the Irish Mission schools, where the Bible was
taught, on pain of eviction; and that Mr. Lavelle had emptied these
schools of the children, and encouraged the people to keep possession of their holdings, though possession of them was demanded by
the Bishop's agents....Lord Plunket was examined—to the question,
whether "In this terrific weather he was purposing to fling seventy
unfortunates on the snow-covered mountains in Partry, and specially,
whether it was really for purposes of *eviction*, and not merely for non-
payment of rent, he had brought these actions," he answered
"*certainly*;" and in several forms he firmly answered that "the sole
object he had in view was to evict these wretched people and drive

Long after Autumn's golden gleams have fled,
And when ungenial scanty rays are shed
Upon the saddened earth, while the weak sun,
Low curving, toward. the farthest south shrinks'
    down
Before the hosts of winter issuing forth,
And pales at the spread pennons of the North,—
When the east-wind pursues a drearier flight,
And fans with colder wings the face of night,—
When Aries sheds down frost-twinkling rays,
While Sirius flashes in the horizon's haze,—
When icy breathings fall among the glens,
And crystals tuft the heaths and rushy fens,—
When the seared oak-leaves, with a chilling sound,
Drive through the rocks or on the hardened
    ground,—·
Or when thick clouds on lofty summits frown,
And torrents swollen with the snows come down,—
When the white drifts along the mountains sweep,
And lowing herds forsake the unsheltered steep,—
When angled lines of famished wildfowl make
For the warm sea, and leave the frozen lake,—
Even when the northern tempest loudly roars—
'Tis then the apostolic wrath outpours :
'Tis then it drives into the deadly air
Its homeless victims straight to meet despair ;

them on the world.... Accepting the uncontradicted facts we can
only say that the conduct of Lord Plunket, in the Partry evictions,
would justify any persecution whatever for conscience sake." Of
course I do not vouch for the evidence attributed to Lord Plunket,
but I have not discovered that he ever published any denial of its
correctness. These, I believe, were the evictions that *The Times*
called " *a hideous scandal.*"

And, Heavens! is it because they still receive
Not that for truth, which they do not believe?
   This dire extermination, undenied,
Has to your MISSION here been long allied;
And rightly now we may those laws debate,
By which our landlords can *exterminate*.—
   No doubt the landlord must in justice get
The value of the land to tenants let.
Some one must *own;* if otherwise, 'tis plain,
All rights should cease and anarchy should reign;
But 'tis as plain, and as the sun in day,
The people should possess the land, and pay:
Their destiny of life is honest toil,
Fulfilled in cultivation of the soil;
And who repress that labor must appear
To think that God should not have sent them
     here.
But no! God gave the land, and lets it fall
To some as landlords for the use of all—
For the whole nation's use; and not, indeed,
That it should rather other countries feed:
As England Irish flocks and herds supply,
Even at the time our starving thousands die.
   A landlord sees the tenant's ripening corn
Around the cabin where his sires were born:
He sees contentment on an earthen floor
And peace and love inside a smoky door;
And honesty is there—for he has got
Each year full payment for the little plot—
And faithfulness; for man and child and wife
Would for a feeling landlord lose their life.

But, in an evil hour, when love of wrong
Gains on the mind, and Satan's force is strong,
The landlord thinks that, by his own good hands,
He can extract more profit from his lands.
It strikes him not he has his share before :
The rankling thought is now—he must have
     more :
He must have *all* that all his land can yield,
And to his own must join the tenant's field.
   The cabin falls; and the unhoused are hurled,
As strangers everywhere, upon the world.
Each hoary bush and sallow-fencing, made
Around the garden, next are prostrate laid ;
And, blest with many a reminiscence dear,
A home and all its features disappear.
O'er the changed scene now cherished oxen pass,
And brutes possess the solitude of grass.
The dismal calls of fattening herds replace
The fireside ditties of an ancient race ;
And bleating flocks o'er the green waste are heard
Where twittered once the merry haggard-bird.
Shame on the direful law that puts away
The honest poor beneath a heartless sway !
And, blest by their own fortune, shame on those
Who make it the curst cause of others' woes !
   Yet many would the wicked system try
With sneerful argument to justify.
" It is the law ;" they say, " as plain as light."
We grant it is *the law ;* but—is it *right?*
" No matter : still it is the law :" they state.
So landlords may indeed exterminate

For lust or vengeance—still reflecting not,
While fixing the poor serf's unhappy lot,
That they themselves, amid their acts abhorred,
Are but the tenants of the eternal Lord,
And with their power o'er the land endued
To turn it to the most extensive good:
But narrowing its good, with hearts of stone
And conscience seared, they make it all their own.
Remorseless, on the tenant they have trod,
Pleased when they broke no law but that of God.
    Yet soon to fear would sink those landlords' rage,
If they indeed *believed* the sacred page,
Forewarning of God's retribution sure
On the exterminators of God's poor,—
Woe unto them, it says, 'gainst mercy steeled,
Who house to house annex, and field to field,
Leaving to charity *no place behind,*
As if the earth was all for them designed.[81]
Men of *high station* thus the Lord offend;
But they shall *meet their judgment* in the end.
Perhaps it is, that they have so oppressed,
No more resources with their victim rest:—
They so *consumed the earnings* of his toil
And *filled their garnished houses with his spoil,*[82]
That now they drive the pauper from their lands,
Heedless of what the *Lord of Hosts* demands:—
What mean ye thus who grind beneath your feet
The faces of the poor, and ye who beat
My people even to pieces ?[83]   Still they stand
Defiant of the Lord's avenging hand,

(81) Isaiah v. 8.   (82) Id. iii. 14.
(83) Id. iii. 15. (Protestant version.)

Inflicting all the miseries they can,
Fearless of God, and not ashamed of man.
And yet more sinfully the heartless tribe
Will even in God's name the poor proscribe;
And of the causes that impel the great
Their honest tenants to exterminate,
The worst is that in which religion blends—
Where impiousness to itself pretends
To act for that just Heaven that it offends.

Indeed your *pastoral crook,* extending toward
The Papist, seldom differed from a sword;
Nor do you now its ancient use reverse,
Wielding it not to gather but disperse.
To have the child by faithless masters taught
The father to a court of law is brought.
There he receives his doom, but still exiled
Prefers to be, when thus he saves his child,
Helped by that God who *turns away his face
From pride,* but to the *humble giveth grace.*[84]
So, *growing worse and worse, seducers* strive
And *erring, would all men to error* DRIVE,[85]
By *might oppressing,* and, with rage replete,
Drawing the poor before the judgment seat.[86]

(85) 2 Tim. iii. 13.

(86) St. James, ii. 6. When the inspired writer speaks in condemnation of those who oppress the poor by bringing them before the judgment seats, he evidently makes a distinction between moral and civil law, and does not, in such cases, admit justification by the latter. This might afford a good theme of reflection to those who seek our conversion from Rome and bring their tenants to law courts by ejectment process.

Thus the apostle wrote; and now in you
We see the sacred words exactly true.
But Oh that each oppressor might be brought
To think, amid the *works* that he has wrought,
Whether the *faith*, of which perhaps he boasts,
May save the judgment of the Lord of Hosts![87]
Or that, indeed, he might reflect before
He lays within the trembling tenant's door
The dread ejectment, whether his commands
May not toward Heaven be held with pitied
    hands!—
As the like missive of the Assyrian dread
Before the Lord King Hezekiah spread.[88]
    And yet in vain is each tyrannic deed
Designed to force the sufferer from his creed.
His breaking heart proclaims your cruel wound,
But, broken, proves the soul within it sound,—
His conscience still superior to distress,
And greater than your strength his feebleness.
    Then unsuccessful is your MISSION still,
With all its promised good and actual ill.
Its varied actions for three hundred years—
Its projects working on our hopes and fears
Have fully failed; and to the present hour
Its zeal remains without persuasive power:
For though among its attributes, bestowed
By the old enemy, opposing God,
The crafty instincts of the snake abound,
Yet serpent-fascination is not found.

(87) St. James ii. 14.

(88) 4 Kings (2 Kings, Protestant Bible) xix. 14.

And wherefore still with acts of rage pursue
Where suffering can only prove men true :
Where a crushed race can, unsubdued, oppose
A faith unbending to tyrannic woes ?
And even when the stricken country pines
In famine, yet this aids not your designs.
Increasing sorrow to our Erin brings
More sheltering folds of guardian angels' wings :
Her faith grows holier in her wasting days,
As the seed ripens while the pulp decays.
And now in higher beauty she excels,
While she declines, and still your arts repels.
With features made more brilliant from above,
Though shrunk in woe, she claims our greater love ;
And, like the tinted foliage, arrayed
More splendidly when leaves in autumn fade,
The drooping form of Erin in distress
Withers, indeed, to brighter loveliness.

True to the end, no power of earth or hell
Can make our Land against her church rebel :
That Church, whose true Catholicism we see
By the quite simple test of unity :
Unshaken in assured perpetual peace
By change to suit Race, climate or caprice :
Plainly the church upon the mountain reared,
That, as Christ promised, never disappeared ;[89]
Built on the mountain, that all men might know
His Temple from afar, and to it flow.[90]
To this we tend, and not to those in sites,
Seen but by few, on mean sectarian heights.

(89) Mat. v. 14.   (90) Is. ii. 2.

But yet the destiny of Christ's church you seek,
And dare to call your creed The Catholic.
If *catholic* means *universal,* how
Must we the title to your church allow?
Declare the reasons that would make us grant
The designation, *even as Protestant:*
Proving that no inquiry can detect,
Among all Protestants, but your one sect.
Yours as their universal church endures!
Therefore its Head and Government are yours.
And if thus Catholic you rightly call
Your Church, its British Head is Head of all.
Yet to this claim would, doubtlessly, demur
All like the Swede, the Dane and Hollander,
Leaving your *Catholicity* to squeeze
Within the limits of the English seas.
Here, certainly, one government is shown;
But now convince us that the *Faith* is one;
Catholic even in one Kingdom thus,
Or even in one District, or one house!
Prove that your universal creed may be
Just universal in one family.
Question each person, and you'll likely find,
Each adds some point, or leaves some point behind.
Few read your dogmas; fewer still conceive
Their drift; and even of those but few believe.
To pass as *Catholic* no fair pretence
You show, though much we may restrict the sense;
And when the name you to yourselves apply,
'Tis but a part of THE TREMENDOUS LIE.

    Then yield at length the envied name to those
In whom the spirit of one doctrine flows;

9

In whose true Catholicity we find
Syntyche and Evodia of one mind;[91]
Whose faith, in every nation, every clime,
And every circumstance and every time,
Displays, in one unseparated light,
No party-colors, and is only bright.
No vain interpreting in tongues of schism;[92]
One Hope; one Faith; one Lord and one baptism;[93]
One mind; one mouth; one Pastor and one flock:[94]
One Church, in fine—the Church upon the rock.[95]

A Church like this alone is catholic;
But yours is not a church even schismatic,
Whose doctrines, scattered upon every wind,[96]
Have left no semblance of *a church* behind.
The *Law-Establishment*, you often call
Your quasi-church, it is; and that is all:—*

(91) Phil. iv. 2.   (92) 1 Cor. xiv. 26.   1 Cor. i. 10.

(93) Eph. iv. 4, 5.   (94) Rom. xv. 6.   S. John x. 16.

(95) S. John xvii. 11.   1 Tim. iii. 15.   S. Mat. xiv. 18.

The Anglican sets little value upon Catholic *Unity* as opposed
to the divided opinions of Protestants; yet in the Book of Common
Prayer we find the following most *Romish* collect, where the holiness
of the Church is made quite dependent on unity:—"O Almighty God,
who hast built thy Church on the foundation of the Apostles and
Prophets, Jesus Christ himself being the head corner-stone, grant
us so to be joined together in unity of spirit by their doctrine, that
we may be made a holy temple acceptable unto thee, through Jesus
Christ our Lord." This Collect is repeated on every SS. Simon and
Jude's day; and on St. Mark's day is said:—"Give us grace, that
being not like little children carried away with every blast of vain
doctrine, we may be established in the truth of thy holy gospel,
through Jesus Christ our Lord."

Here is sound Catholic doctrine embraced by Anglicanism, yet
opposed by Anglicans: and it may be added to those wondrous
contradictions referred to in previous notes.

(96) Eph. iv. 14.   * See additional note E.

A Church that to the self-same law resorts
For guaranty of tenets and supports.
And now to that support you so pursue—
The so-called *Rent-charge*—let us turn our view,
Canvass its state, and see how well from thence
You draw a claim on Papists' reverence.—

For years and years the furious falchion glowed
Of the Tithes - fiend: our blood in torrents
    flowed:
His wealth extracted from the shrieking poor;
But when the victim could no more endure,
The tax was settled in another way,
And lessened when the rich had all to pay.
Now it is argued—" men must clearly see
The present *Rent-charge* can no grievance be.
No part is taken from the poor man's hands:
'Tis all a rent of landlords for their lands.
Therefore the papist landlord, who must pay,
Against the impost ought not to inveigh.
He bought his land, suppose; but, then, before
He bought, it paid the charge. He pays no more;
And so the landlord now endures no wrong,
Who pays what never did to him belong.
The Rent-charge with his land he did not buy."
Quite true! But here's the question now to try:—
The "charge" is not the landlord's like the land;
But is it then the parson's, we demand?
Long before parsons preached, the tithe-charge
    stood
To aid the people's church and public good.
How then to a new sect has passed the claim,
Where still the people's church remains the same?

Say can you prove the transfer thus to be
Other than the most base iniquity?
You cannot surely, and in reason's sight,
The parson vainly seeks a *genuine* right.
He grasps the " charge" by *legal* right, because
Here laws made conscience, and not conscience laws.

    By that one sign, if not one more were known,
Your system's falseness would be fully shown.
For what but falseness in it can there be,
When its support is plain dishonesty?
Yet other signs there are of dismal shade
By which your falseness is as well betrayed.—
And, still apart from tenets, while we see
Among your *proselyting* ministry,
That slanderous tongues belie your white cravats,
And pride and heartlessness, your shovel-hats,
The fame of truth no thinking man will yield
To this hypocrisy so ill concealed.
And while you circulate, with labor hard,
Tracts by the ton and libels by the yard,
And prove the ardor, whose untired monition
Secures old dames' subscriptions for the MISSION—
While we observe the pulpit zeal that strives
To win gray sinners' hearts or young rich wives,[97]

    (97) That matrimonial success is often a stimulant of Anglican
pulpit zeal is a matter of notoriety. It is so much so that we cannot
be surprised at marrying parsons advertising themselves. The
Edinburgh Review, No. 200, page 293, gives us an example taken from
the *Record*. In the advertisement in question the clergyman sets
himself out as desiring a sole charge in some town sphere of useful-
ness, and states that he is a *bachelor*, of high qualifications, desiring
good society and a suitable stipend.

And know, among both sexes, your eclat,
Gained by religious airs *et cetera*,
Still are we not about your church misled;
And, bravely as it lifts its lofty head,
We yet pronounce it, in its clear addiction
To worldliness, at bottom but a fiction.
Such falseness show the airy hills that rise,
Lit by the sunset in wild wintry skies.
Like snowy Alps we see their summits proud;
But view their base : there they are plainly cloud.

Yet you succeed, you may, perhaps, assert,
The faith of some odd catholic to subvert.
With some weak minds, indeed, you might
    achieve
The blest result—to make them *unbelieve.*
Working on their poor reason, you might scath
Belief in matters held by Christian Faith.
They *know* that *you* are wrong; and then as well
To doubt themselves you might those minds
    impel.
But drive the soul *from Rome,* and then you care
Not how it wanders, when it stays not there;
And thus Rome's doctrines you abuse alone,
Not showing still the soundness of your own,—
Telling the catholic he goes astray,
Yet leaving him unsure of the right way ;
And as a convert you would have him prized,
To Deism simply full *un-Romanized.*

Not to our "errors" still you seem to be
Such foes as to our Head and Unity.
At first the *Pope* appeared the greatest ill
Reformers saw, and so they see him still.

And in the present time, when dangers rise
Around his throne bedimmed by lowering skies,
At the near prospect of its doom elate,
The Papacy's extinction you await.
You think, if Pius lost his temporal crown
His spiritual too should be pulled down.
But vain the cherished hope; and yet we grant
The hope is proper in a Protestant;
For, while you draw not the distinctive line,
In man, 'tween earthly power and power divine,
Among your princes this on that depends;
So if that fails the other surely ends.
Hence you display no separate crowns employed,
But two in one have mutually alloyed.
But the Pope's crown of spiritual might
Is different from that of temporal right;
Nor are they, because long and closely linked,
Therefore less independent and distinct.
Man, who gave one, that one might take away;
Still heavenly beams would on the other play.
Think not, if fails its temporal defence,
The Papacy must fall by consequence:
For, unattainable by earth or hell,
It still shall hold its heavenly citadel;
And men might reach the sky by Babel's tower
As soon as subjugate the Pope's true power.

  Against the throne of Pius to prevail,
Means, therefore, not that Peter's chair will
      fail;
And, spite of what the hating bigot saith,
And Catholics may fear in feeble faith,

While time remains,—while day divides from
    night,—
While planets speed around each central light,
And suns themselves with eddying systems run
Round the great universal centre's sun,—
While Earth's astronomers, with anxious eyes,
See constellations widening on the skies,
Or even mark their stars more closely cast
Together, when we move advancing past,
Unbroken still the Papal line shall last.

    And not, indeed, until destruction's pall
Shall spread o'er Nature at the Trumpet's call,—
Until the powers of dissolution brood
On day's dimmed orb and on the moon of blood,—
Not until time shall cease and death shall die,
And Heaven descending light the sunless sky,
Shall Peter's last Successor, at the feet
Of Christ, resign his charge before the Judgment
    Seat.

    Now if we err in saying you pretend
Religion for a base and worldly end,
And if, in truth, you may sincerely claim
Pure Gospel doctrine as your MISSION's aim,
Before you reasonably can expect
The faith of injured Ireland to direct,
You must be able perfectly to prove
That Gospel doctrine is not one of love,—
That Spoliation is a Christian calling,
And Mammon's spirit keeps the soul from
    falling,—
That pride is vouchsafed by Almighty grace,
And luxury ensures a heavenly place,—

That from the Saviour hatred must descend,
And that his Church must on the State depend,—
That Antichrist must surely be put down
By faith that's subject to the British crown,—
That the Divine Religion, to endure,
Must rest on common law and sinecure,—
That Doctrine must be surely counted good,
When by its followers not understood ;
And subject to be variously expounded,
Betrays with what perfection it was founded.
You must, still further, make us plainly see,
Divine support *disproved by Unity,*
And show that when a Faith remains unchanged,
It then is, doubtless, from the Lord estranged,—
That influence with mankind and extent
Is for a sign of God's disfavor meant,—
That when, in short, a Doctrine can lay claim,
With truth, to being ever still the same,
Not in one age nor country, but in all,
It only manifests its doom to fall.—
All this established, you may well proceed,
With hope, to draw us from our ancient Creed.
We *then* may see full reason to believe
That church-expounded doctrine may deceive,
And that the old Apostles of each nation
Were English-churchmen by anticipation.
We *then* may venerate the MISSION'S zeal
That flashed of old from desolating steel,
Persuaded that the dread chastising sword,
Which scourged our land, was truly of the Lord,
And where the raging MISSIONARY killed,
That there the Gospel's precepts were fulfilled.

When deeds of slaughter we shall thus revere,
Rapine and waste shall not less blest appear.
We shall no longer blame the wrathful hands,
That wide with hallowed ruins strewed our lands;
No longer grieve among the mouldering walls
And grass-grown floors of ancient sacred halls,
Viewing the altar with its mossy stains,
Swept by the storms and by the snows and rains;
Nor shall we mourn the crumbling bell-tower drest
In the sad beauties of its ivy vest.—
No pang of sorrow then shall touch the heart,
Where rude defacement spoils the Sculptor's art;
Nor still shall tasteful piety repine
At broken font or devastated shrine,
Or cross thrown down, now by rank weeds o'er-
    grown—
Once raised above where charity fixed her throne;
Nor shall we learning's fallen seats lament,
Whence light o'er Europe in dark ages went—
Those seats, one time our land's proud evidence
Of living glory,—now its monuments.[98]

(98) The ancient learning of Ireland and her large share in the
christianizing of Europe are universally acknowledged. A writer in
Chambers' Edinburgh Journal (No. 160. New Series) contrasts the
present state of Ireland with its former wealth, literature, and refinement, as indicated by the surprizing number of objects of antiquity
that are found there, and says—"You see the remains of ecclesiastical
edifices with the most gorgeous carvings; stone crosses lying prone
in the dust, any one of which would be the marvel of an English
county, and in museums you are shown books of vellum in the ancient
Irish character, bound in gold and silver, and ornamented with
precious stones, which are said to be worth, in the present day
thousands of pounds..... The Irish, though possessing no individual
history, would nevertheless appear to have been at one period the

No more, then, shall indignant grief inflame
Amid those wrecked mementos of our fame;
But rather, in the desolator's praise,
The voice of gratitude we shall upraise.
When the free sunlight through the gable falls
We shall laud ruin in the fissured walls,
And, during nightly doleful cries and howls,
Bless those who gave them to the winds and
        owls.
True Gospel fervor we shall understand
In plundering of tithes and of church-land.
We may rejoice, too, that you wiped away
Each charge that the first owners had to pay:—
The ever ready hospitable board,
And comforts for the weary traveller stored:
The education that they should secure
To Christian youth: the maintenance of the Poor.
And we may gladden at each act we see
Even still suppressive of the monkery
That, unsupported by church-lands or rates,
Relieves the destitute and educates.

most learned nation in Europe. Egypt, Greece, Rome, Ireland—these
seem to have been the countries in which learning of a refined nature
progressively found refuge and repose. The manner in which the
civilization of each was in turn laid prostrate was the same. Egypt
was in part despoiled by Greece; Greece was similarly despoiled by
Rome; Rome was despoiled by the Teutonic nations of the north;
and two branches of those nations, the Danes and Anglo-Normans,
completed the train of ruination by despoiling Ireland.....In this
view of affairs, Ireland is to England what Greece was to Rome—the
spot whence it derived not a little of its civilization, and which it
afterwards maltreated in requital. In a word, and in all seriousness,
IRELAND IS THE GREECE OF THE BRITISH ISLANDS." The great
Humboldt, in his Cosmos, points out that the germs of the
Copernican astronomy are found in the writings of an Irish monk.

Thus we may praise the landlord-pastoral crooks
Ejecting it, its charities and books;[99]
And when the landlord ruthlessly expels
The tenant in whose bosom conscience dwells,
And hence who awful mandates disobeys,
Saving his faith, we shall no censure raise.
  In fine—when acts of virtue we can see
In all your deeds of various tyranny
For centuries, while rapine's lust and hate
Now shed our blood, and now "exterminate,"—
When we can hope to hear true Christian laws
Amid our woe from those who are its cause,
And when the proofs of truth we now esteem
Can even as the marks of falseness seem,
Then by new courses we shall Faith pursue,
Guided by MAMMON, BELIAL AND YOU.

(99) The reader will probably be reminded here of Lord Plunket's celebrated ejectment of the *Christian Brothers* from their educational establishment in Tuam.

THE END.

ADDITIONAL NOTES.

NOTE A.

The moral effects of the Reformation in England may be gathered from its apologist and historian *Burnet*, from whom I will quote a few passages on the subject. He says—"There was at that time [King Edward's Reign] a very scandalous venality in all offices and employments, which was so much talked of at the court of France..and it was said that whereas King Henry had by his endowments made some restitution, yet for all the wealth they had seized on in chantries and collegiate churches, no schools or hospitals were yet endowed." He goes on to tell us of Ridley's complaint that the king was about giving a Prebend in St. Paul's for the furniture of his stable, which makes Ridley ask, "Is this the fruit of the Gospel?" He next informs us of a charge "made by one Norman against the Archbishop of York, that he took his wife and kept her from him," resulting in the Archbishop being forbidden to come to Parliament. The worthy Archbishop (Holgate) is described, as *heartily concurring in the reformation* [not a doubt of it!] but he was looked on rather as a reproach to it than a promoter. We are then told of King Edward's opinion of the bishops of that time; the supreme Head declaring that, "some for sloth, some for ignorance, some for luxury and some for popery are unfit for discipline and government." (Hist. of the Reform. Bohn's 8vo. Ed. 1857. p. 757.) After relating a family legend about the Archbishop of Armagh and a monk who drank to him in a poisoned liquor of which they both died, Burnet tells us that the death of King Edward was looked on by all people "as a just judgment of God upon those who pretended to love and promote a Reformation, but whose impious and flagitious lives were a reproach to it. The open lewdness in which many lived without shame or remorse gave great occasion to their adversaries to say that they were in the right to assert justification by faith without works, since they were, as to every good work, reprobate. Their gross and insatiable scrambling after the goods and wealth that had been dedicated with good designs, though to superstitious uses, without applying any part of it to promoting the gospel, the instructing the

youth and relieving the poor, made all people conclude that it was
for robbery, and not for reformation, that their zeal made them so
active." Burnet then gives an account of certain *fraudulent* proceedings carried on for the pretended *advancement of God's glory* [the
common cant] and informs us that the irregular and immoral lives
of many of the professors of the gospel gave their enemies great
advantages to say, they ran away from confession, penance, fasting
and prayers, only that they might be under no restraint, but indulge
themselves in a licentious and dissolute course of life. By these
things, that were but too visible *in some of the more eminent among
them*, the people were much alienated from them: and as much as
they were formerly prejudiced against popery, *they grew to have
kinder thoughts of it*, and to look on all changes that had been made,
as designs to enrich some vicious courtiers, and to let in an inunda-
tion of vice and wickedness upon the nation." He then affirms that
there were great and shining lights among them, but "they were few
in comparison of the many bad," and in comparison with those in
whom the old leaven had still a deep root, who were insincere in
their professions of faith, and discontented at getting nothing for
their subsistence in lieu of their perquisites at masses and other
practices. He continues:—"That which was above all was, that
God was highly dishonoured by men who pretended zeal for his glory
but with their works dishonoured him. They talked of the purity of
the Gospel, while they were wallowing in all sensuality and unclean-
ness: *pretending to put all their confidence in the merits and sufferings
of Christ*, while they were crucifying him afresh and putting him to
open shame....They were men in whose hands things grew every day
worse and worse; and whose arrogance and other disorders our chief
reformers were forced in some measure to connive at, that they might
not provoke them to retard a work that *could in no wise be carried on
without their countenance and authority*." What a pity to see Heaven
so quite at the mercy of such men !

But what were the effects of the Reformation in Burnet's own
time, 150 years afterwards? He tells us ;—"To the viciousness of
life, and the open immoralities and neglect of religion that were the
sins of a former age, many among us have added a studied impiety,
and a laboured opposition to all revealed religion, which some have
owned in so barefaced a manner, that perhaps no age of the world
can show anything like it. If others *with secular views* have declaim-
ed against this, and put on some show of zeal, how much more of
party than true religion has appeared in it. The divided parties
among us have showed little true regard to religion and to a course
of virtue and piety, &c." So it appears that at that time the friends

of religion were those who took its part from secular views. A hopeful growth, truly, of 150 years!

Our author complains of the venality of the advowsons and the little attempt made to throw out abuses and restore discipline, and exclaims—"How few do fast and pray....that so we may by our intercessions, deliver our church and our nation from that which is ready to swallow us up." He concludes, after all, with a reflection, which makes him hope that the Reformation was under the care of Providence! (Ib. pp. 770, 771, 772). The *Hist. of his own Time*, by the same author, is full of animadversions on the Protestant clergy. In a lecture to them (Conclusion, p. 382, Fol, Ed. 1734) he again recommends fasting, *at least once a quarter in Ember week*, and it is not unworthy of remark that in the same sentence he desires them to get by heart certain passages in the Epistles to Timothy and Titus, though we know that one of those is *now* turned against the Catholics for *their* fasting. A little afterwards he says—"Indeed I have lamented during my whole life that I saw so little true zeal among our clergy: *I saw much of it among the clergy of Rome* though it is both ill directed and ill conducted;" and he shows that he has an eye to the main point, when he encourages the Anglican clergymen to attend to his general advice by assuring them, that he "never knew any one who conducted himself by these rules, but he was brought *into good posts, or at least into an easy state of subsistence.*" No wonder that this state of the early Anglican Church should tend to the perfect confusion in the Establishment, and the demoralization of the people, which we see in our own times.

The state of society in England in 1856, was thus briefly described by the *Court Service Gazette.*

"We have a Society for promoting Christianity among the Jews. Give us a Society for Promoting Christianity amongst Christians.—The most hideous atrocities occur in the blaze of open day. Men are thugged and garotted in the streets of London; the 'villanous centre-bit' of the burglar, as Mr. Tennyson aptly calls it, grates on the waking ear of the trembling tenant; our ticket-of-leave men are prowling about like wolves; the Pagan virtues of fair play and fair dealing are vanishing from among us; trade has become a matter of trickery—your grocer does not care a bean-blossom though he poison you, so that before you die he may turn you to some profit by putting *nux vomica* in your porter, acetate of lead in your gin, hydrate of lime in your flour, sulphuric acid in your vinegar, and the bisulphuret of mercury in your snuff. The *Times* deplores the want of "a proper spirit in our merchants and traders"—that proper spirit being the old, now obsolete, quality of common honesty. Ah!

but still worse remains behind. The blood of murdered men and women cries to Heaven for vengeance. The Burdon murder—the Islington murder—the Minories murder—the Burnopfield murder—the Maidstone murder—the Southampton murder—the Rugeley murder—on they come in grim and ghastly array; and what embarrasses the newspaper reader and perplexes him beyond all measure, is to keep these frightful occurrences distinct in his memory, so as not to confound the characters and incidents of one tragedy with those of another. Yes, say what you will, this is the age of iron. While we have been painting the figure-head the ship has run upon a rock—already there are five feet of water in the hold."

That matters have not improved in later years, may be seen by the following comments of the *Morning Post* of August 14th, 1860, on the judge's charge when opening the Assizes at Liverpool:—

" Never before, says Baron Martin, in the course of his whole judicial experience, has he seen so heavy a calendar. With the single exception of treason, it enjoys the unenviable distinction of embracing every crime under heaven which can render a man obnoxious to the laws of England. Four murders, fourteen cases of manslaughter, twenty-four of burglary, are among the products of this ominous jail delivery. Robbery, stabbing, and a host of minor offences have all their separate representatives. If we need any stimulus to increased exertion in the cause of morality, it is amply supplied by the list of prisoners undergoing their trial at the present moment in one county town alone. Little flattering as the conclusion may be to our national vanity, *we doubt whether the Liverpool calendar be not a very tolerable index of the state 'of crime all over the country.* Within a few weeks we have been called upon to chronicle a succession of homicides, or attempted homicides, alike repulsive in their barbarous details, and apparently destitute of any adequate incentives. The wretched child who fell a victim to the knife of the assassin in an obscure Wiltshire village could scarcely have excited the resentment of his murderer, and might even have been supposed to be safe from his fears. We have had one case in which a few angry words between two fellow servants at a lonely farm on a Cumberland hill side resulted in the deliberate butchery of a female. Another woman was sent to her last account in consequence of a lovers' quarrel, originating in an ineffectual attempt upon the part of her admirer to tender some good advice. Its ill reception by the object of his affections piqued him, and the death of the girl was apparently the only thing which could give relief to his wounded feelings. A still darker tragedy yet awaits investigation at the hands of justice. A single night proved fatal in one of the suburbs of the metropolis itself to no less than four unoffending individuals. Of five inmates of the dwelling one alone survives. Mother; brothers, and affianced bride, all perished undoubtedly by the same knife. While such things can still occur at our very doors, it is vain to plume ourselves upon a civilization and refinement which yet abound with passages worthy of the recent savage episodes of the Lebanon or Damascus."

The *Times* of Dec. 26, 1860, tells us that there were only five convictions for homicides during the year in all Ireland, whose happy state it ascribes to the *tender care* of England: that is, to the care of the country whose own moral condition has been described as above by Baron Martin and the *Morning Post!* Here it may be remarked, that, in its article on the decrease of the Irish population, as shown by the Census of 1861, the *Times* says nothing of *the tender care of England.*

Some idea of the state of society among the upper classes may be gathered from the "Belgravian Lament" correspondence contained in the *Times* of June 27, 1861, and subsequent numbers of that paper. The correspondent of the *Liverpool Albion*, writing on this subject, remarks :—" The Millennium of the pessimists appears to be approaching ; and in the evaporation of public virtue and the growth of private vice, and the general insensibility to both, may be contemplated a reproduction of portents that have invariably heralded the decadence of empire."

" We have lately been breakfasting full of horrors," exclaims the *Times* of July 23, 1861 ; " ....that such crimes must be, we are told by the annals of all ages and countries ; but need they abound as they do, and that not in the uneducated, the neglected and the starving, but in those respectable middle classes, which are the pride, and, as many think, the staple of England ?"

The *Weekly Times* of Nov. 24, 1861, commenting on the spirit of English murder, says :—"No age has been exempt from it. Youths, mature and old men have barbarously murdered, and women have destroyed in numbers their own offspring. This dreadful disregard of life must spring from some general cause. The idea of a future existence and its responsibilities may have been weakened. The bringing up of children may have been more abandoned and neglected. The stimulants of drink may have indurated the mind, and stimulated the brutal passions. Whatever cause we may assign it to, the terrible fact stares us in the face, that murder, cold-blooded, premeditated, determined murder, is frequent among us."

The people of Ireland are called " *Thugs*" by English writers on account of the agrarian murders that are committed there from time to time in certain districts, but beside the unfairness of abusing an entire country for the crimes of a part, it may be said that neither in number nor in character can they be compared with the murders that disgrace England. The Irish murderer's motive is *revenge*, and, though this, of course, does not excuse the offence, we may safely assert that it is far surpassed in atrocity by that which springs from the incentives of lust or avarice or from the simple desire of spilling blood. These are the motives of the English murderer, who often in his own family seeks his victim; and it may be the poisoned parent, the strangled wife, or the child stabbed to death that will afford the breakfast of horror described by the *Times*. In Ireland murders of this description are rare indeed; and in which country will the unprejudiced observer say that the *spirit* of murder—the *true thuggism*—is more apparent,—here, where the judicial strangulation is witnessed with horror and where the spectators join in prayer for the wretched criminal, or in England, where the execution is witnessed with blasphemy, obscenity and levity of the most revolting character?

The way in which an English crowd enjoy the feast of death was ably described by the *Daily Telegraph* of Oct. 21, 1862, in its account of the execution of Catherine Wilson, a woman, who, with almost her last breath, protested her innocence. "The cry of 'hats off!'" says the *Telegraph*, "about ten minutes before the eagerly looked for time, arose with a fierce vehemence and was followed by the sight of hats and caps flying through the air in all directions. Still the roar of the crowd continued; and shrill laughs and patches of song broke now and then on the hoarse diapason of blasphemous ribaldry." The *dress* of the wretched creature, as the hangman completed her ghastly toilet by drawing a long white cap over her head, furnished an ample fund of merriment to the brutal concourse, and, finally, "if any sort of compassion had been felt by the multitude at the very moment of their savage mirth, it was soon forgotten. The crowd broke up with loud yells and whoops of laughter."

Again, Irishmen are called *Thugs* on account of the faction fights that occur within a very limited district. [See *The Times* of Nov. 11, 1862.] We cannot sufficiently deplore this lingering spirit of ancient clanship; but the loss of life that it occasions is surely not to be compared to the manslaughters that are of almost daily occurrence in England. Neither is it over modest in Englishmen to call the excited faction fighter a *Thug* as long as they coolly gamble away human life in the prize-ring, and prove in the frequent results of the game laws that they regard it as of less value than that of hares or partridges.

NOTE B.

THE STATE OF RELIGION IN ENGLAND may not improperly be inquired into by those who are so importuned to exchange their Catholic faith for Anglican doctrines. I am therefore induced to compile a rather lengthy note made out from various publications; and, I may observe, that *I carefully avoid quoting any " Romish" authority.*

Many of us remember the appeal for aid published in the *Times* by the Rev. Mr. Stock, Protestant Incumbent of the district of All Saints, Islington, which he says " with a poor population of nearly 20,000, has but one small church, a sunday school and an infant school; as might be expected, therefore, Socialism, Infidelity, Rationalism and indifference, prevail in every quarter to a fearful extent." Mr. Stock gives examples of the replies of different persons spoken to by the Clergy and Scripture Readers.

One answer will suffice to show the use to which the Anglican Bible is turned, and its perfection as the *sole rule of faith* among the people :—

1. " —— has been to church twice in eighteen years : spends Sundays in a beer-shop. Occasionally a Bible is produced that passages, apparently opposed to each other, may be compared. An appeal is then made to the party whether such a book can be from God, and it is condemned as a ' pack of lies.' "

In the Public worship (Census, England and Wales) Report of 1851, we find many facts not flattering to national religion. The "labouring myriads" are described as not less strangers to religious ordinances than the people of a heathen country, (p. clviii.) and by natural inclination adverse to the entertainment of religious sentiments, but still retaining a vague sense of some tremendous want which ought to encourage the labours of zealous preachers. A sad proof that " the masses are by no means inaccessible to earnest importunity" is seen in the progress of the Mormon faith, and it only requires a zeal on the part of the orthodox evangelists equal to that of the Mormon "prophets" and "apostles" to bring the dim unsatisfied religious aspirations of the people to an orthodox belief. (p. clxii). The Report shows that although the Church accommodation in England is insufficient for all who *could* attend public worship, still it is vastly greater than is necessary for those who *do* attend ; that " the greatest difficulty is to fill the churches when provided ; and that this can only be accomplished by a great addition to the number of efficient, earnest, religious *teachers*, clerical or lay, by *whose persuasions the reluctant population might be won.*" (p.

clxvii.) And still our Anglican Missionaries would rather try to disturb the poor Irish in their Catholic faith than assist at the evangelizing of England!

In January 1856, *The Record* Newspaper, one of the chief Protestant organs, called for united prayer on the then approaching Session of Parliament, saying, that " Our national observance of the Lord's-day, in a few weeks or months, will be exposed to peculiar jeopardy. Disorganized influences of all kinds are at work in our intellectual circles. A wide-spread haziness, a dreamy, misty no creed is very largely blotting out the knowledge of the plainest truths of the Gospel, or the fundamental laws of national obligation. Nothing less than a firm grasp on the truths of Scripture, in their whole length and breadth, is likely to bear the strain of sceptical doubt, the ebb and tide of a surging chaos of opinions, to which the rising generation are now exposed."

A report made by the Rev. N. H. Pilkington, Chaplain of Walsingham Bridewell, describes " the awful, almost incredible ignorance of the agricultural classes in this district of Norfolk." During the past year 210 prisoners were committed to the bridewell, and of these, 121 could not read a letter in a book, 157 could not write their names, 57 could not say a word of the Lord's Prayer, and 84 could say it but very imperfectly, 61 could not tell who Jesus Christ was, nor state how or for what purpose He died, and were, " to all intents and purposes, heathens, being ignorant of the simplest and commonest Christian truths .... Many who could say the Lord's Prayer, said it by rote, without knowing its meaning or why it was so called. Many of them had been at school when children, some even for three or four years, but having been early removed, and from that time uncared for, very soon forgot what they had learnt, and in a short time became perfect heathens, not only practically but intellectually." Mr. Pilkington strongly recommends adult evening schools " as the best means of checking and counteracting such a melancholy state of things."

The state of English religion in 1861, was well described by the Rev. R. M. Wilcox, at a meeting of the Southwark Home Missionary Association, held on the 15th of February. I give a few extracts from his Report as Local Secretary, as it appeared in *The Dial* of February 22:

The rev. gentleman quoted the following remarks of Mr. (afterwards Dr.) Harris, made twenty years ago, as still, in the main, applicable — but to a vastly increased population — in London. " What is their state?" (that is, of the mass of the people). "It is a condensed mass of heathenism, which, if drawn out and diffused

over a large space in which it could be examined in detail, would
amaze and alarm you into benevolent activity. What is their state !
It is a concentration of depravity so virulent that it might suffice to
inoculate a continent—a world—with vice. What is their state ! It
is as bad as the most perfect system of evil which the Tempter could
devise, and keep in constant operation with no other law than the
feeble voice of human law can make to it."

After giving some statistics of crime, Mr. Wilcox continued—

"The same terrible state prevailed, in proportion, in all our large
provincial towns, and required enlarged Christian activity to con -
front and conquer—by the Holy Ghost—by love unfeigned—by the
Word of Truth—by the armour of righteousness on the right hand
and on the left. The agricultural portion of our population—while
behind the dense masses of the towns in information—were not a
whit less irreligious or immoral; and there was sad and sufficient
reason for the statement in the recent report on religious worship :
' The myriads of our labouring population, really as ignorant of
Christianity as were the heathen Saxons at Augustine's landing, are
as much in need of missionary enterprise to bring them into prac-
tical acquaintance with its doctrines.' The noblest phase of Christian life was Christian patriotism. In conclusion, he called on those
who were animated by the Spirit of Christ singly and collectively
to put forth their divinely-energised capabilities for the evangelisation of their fellow-countrymen."

At a Methodist Meeting at City Road Chapel, reported in *The
Dial* of Feb. 1, it was resolved :—

"That this meeting, deploring the large amount of home heathenism which prevails amongst both our urban and rural populations,
promises, in the strength of Divine grace, to aid, by personal effort,
by pecuniary contributions, and by prayer to God for the outpouring
of His Holy Spirit, the work of home evangelisation."

Religion among the masses is evidently not improving; and among
the learned of the Church, it is either relapsing into "Popery," or
becoming quite extinguished, "oscillating," as a late Protestant
writer affirms, "from Romanism to Rationalism," or, as he more
charitably defines it, "from *Babylon* to *Babel*." [See pamphlet by
the Rev. John Cairns, on the subject of the *Essays and Reviews*,
pp. 1 and 17]. Without perceiving that what he laments is but a
natural consequence of the Reformation, Dr. Cairns speaks of the
divergent paths, the divisions, the successive stages of Theism, Pantheism or worse, the conflicting paradoxes in speculation, the example of Germany [that cradle of the Reformation] in Rationalism, as
applying to the present movement in the Church, and says that

"The wedge which rends asunder the Christian religion can hardly save the integrity of the Church of England." (p. 19). I may here observe that if the Rev. Doctor had learned to see "*the* Christian religion" in the Church he defines as "Babylon," he would find no wedge rending it asunder.

But the wedge is sinking deeply into reformed Christianity, and not deeper into any of its branches than into Anglicanism ; for it is admitted, as the *Daily News* informs us, (February 12, 1861), that "all forms of religious doctrine, from the highest Calvinism to the lowest Rationalism, are both tolerated and publicly taught in the Church of England."

A correspondent of the *Record* rejoices that "at least one of our bishops has made a bold stand against the great evils that now threaten our Church," and states, that the Bishop of Winchester, at an ordination held by him, "expressly framed his examination to meet most pointedly the great questions of the atonement, and the sufficiency, and inspiration of the Holy Scripture," and declared that he would never knowingly ordain any one holding views approaching to those advocated by the writers of the notorious "Essays and Reviews." This shows the progress of those ideas among the clergy and the candidates for holy orders. (*Record* of December 26, 1860.)

The *Record* of November 16, 1860, in a review of a work by the Rev. D. Wilson, declares its thankfulness for the lifting up of a rallying signal against the progress of Neologian error, and pronounces the pamphlet as useful against "the negative theology so rife in the current literature of the day, and also, alas! in the teachings at our universities." In a leading article of December 10, the *Record* says, "The *Essays* and such like works are being read with avidity by our educated men in and out of the universities. They are leavening the tone of thought, loosening the hold of authority, creating disbelief of creeds and articles, and reducing the very central truths of Christianity to the level of mere human opinions." At a meeting of the clergy held in the Great Hall, Sion College, London Wall, the Rev. Dr. McCaul moved an address to the bishop on "the necessity of some steps being adopted by the rulers of the Church of England to stem the tide of infidelity setting in, which was the more dangerous as not proceeding from open enemies, but from gentlemen holding high spiritual and educational offices in connection with the Established Church of this country." (See *Dial* of February 1, 1861.) This was well intended, no doubt ; but what effective steps *could* be adopted in "a Church," as the *Dial*, A CHURCH OF ENGLAND JOURNAL, remarks, "declared to have no rulers and no belief ?"

An address to the clergy by Archdeacon Coxe, noticed in a Durham newspaper, describes in more vivid colours the spread of infidelity among the clergy, and deplores " the Bible so ruthlessly assailed and so tamely defended." The archdeacon, alluding to the infidel opinions of teachers in the Church, asks sorrowfully, "what is the Church's faith?"—a very pertinent question, that we, Catholics, have been ever asking those who want to convert us.

In the prospectus of a " new Evangelical Church newspaper, *The Compass*," we read that " a new crisis of controversy has arrived to the Church. Opinion, reaching from an untenable and intolerable sacerdotalism, has oscillated to a desperate extreme. Ecclesiastical unity is disturbed by the boldest heterodoxy. Existing clerical and religious associations are threatened with change; and the occasion is appropriate for the publication of a journal for Evangelical Churchmen, which shall supply the long felt deficiency. The scandal is too notorious, and the disaster too tremendous, that the national Church of England should become an organized hypocrisy indeed, and permit sacerdotalism, Pantheism, and Atheism, thinly masked, to subscribe her Evangelical standards of faith, enjoy her emoluments and honours, and minister in her congregations in the name of the One Lord Jesus Christ. But England is too honest, if honestly appealed to, long to remain inactive or obstructive, whenever righteous efforts, without partiality and without hypocrisy, shall be genuinely made to render her National Reformed Church a fountain of pure truth, instead of a mingling pool of muddy and poisonous waters. The days for sham manœuvrings are past. The Church must be purified."

A remarkable book, entitled *Travels in England*, by Dr. Shaw, (published, 1861) affords information not very encouraging to the exchange of our ancient creed for the principles of the English Reformation. The author is evidently no friend of Irishmen or "Popery;" a fact that has induced me the more to give quotations from his work, in which will be found a picture of misery and social degradation, such as no part of Christendom could, perhaps, afford, except the country that he describes.

Speaking of the rich yeomen and tenants, he says, "With many of them life is one career of eating, drinking, visiting, smoking, and sensual enjoyment; they are mere animals with no higher sense of enjoyment." (page 74.) Yet they are not without the organ of veneration, for "in no part of the world that I have visited, is money and rank so thoroughly worshipped as in this." (p. 76.) Describing particular localities, Dr. Shaw begins with London, where, out of 37,000 Welsh residents, 28,000 attend no place of worship at all. Infidelity, in all its degrees, prevails among them. Some have become avowed Papists. Cases of immorality are found which, from their enormity cannot be specified in a public report. Many of the parties, guilty of those enormities, are ignorant of the very first elements of religion. (p. 87) At Hampstead, only a few have the form of religion. (p. 88.) The cardinal truths of the Gospel are certainly not generally received by the people, and are almost as well understood by the Heathens." (p. 89)

Dr. Shaw says that the "unusual amount of Irish in Liverpool, many of them grossly ignorant, tends not a little to make the place worse than it otherwise would be;" but Liverpool, bad as it is, contrasts favorably indeed with Brighton; a place celebrated for its displays of wealth and fashion, and one peculiarly free from the Doctor's Irish element of degradation. Here he saw sights that proved the existence, to an alarming extent, of semi-barbarism, and even heathenism itself. (p. 151.) I wish the admirers of those English humorists, who rally the Irish about their dunghills and their pigs, would read *Dr. Shaw's Travels in England.* Describing some parts of fashionable Brighton, after alluding to the difficulty he experienced in trying to choose his steps through the filth, he says: "The diminutive size of the houses, combined with their ill-ventilation and want of light, render them unfit for cows to live in, and the missionary [Dr. Shaw's companion] frequently cautioned me to touch nothing for fear of carrying away vermin. I said to an old woman, ' How long is it since you have seen the clergyman of the parish ?'

' Why, Sir, not for these last seven years.' " (p. 155.)

To hear a sermon from the Doctor's companion, the wretched people " left their haunts, as worms quit their holes at the approach of a shower, to have their ears tickled with something new and fresh ; they came out, like reptiles after a thunder-storm, from their old and slimy habitations to be refreshed, or else to ridicule the solemn word of exhortation that was addressed to them." (p. 160.) In Bristol " it is considered quite a victory to induce a person from some neighbourhoods to go to a place of worship." (p. 166.) Here Dr. Shaw met with more uneducated people than he had previously seen in England, and he asks the people, " why do they not imitate Liverpool ?" notwithstanding its Irish character, which he complains of. In parts of the fashionable town of Bath, " such is the heathenism and immoral condition of the people, that some of them have never attended a place of worship since their children were christened." " Among a population of 2,000 in the neighbourhood of Avon Street, only 200 attend a place of worship." (p. 168.) "A missionary, on entering a court, found the people as low and degraded as sin and vice could make them, living in filth and wretchedness. Not one that he visited had ever gone to church or chapel." There are some Irish families in Bath, and what does the missionary say of them? They declined his visits and his tracts, certainly; but was it on the same grounds as the English infidels? No, thank Heaven: "they told him not to trouble them, as they had a priest to take care of their souls;" and "put their fingers in their ears, saying, 'don't hear him—ours is the true religion—he don't know anything about it.'" Yet the missionary asserts that "the priests appear to care very little about them," and concludes his revenge for the repulse by speaking in contemptuous terms of the Sacrament of Extreme Unction. (pp. 170, 173.) In page 179 Dr. Shaw tells us that "an awful mass of humanity that lives in these islands have never heard this mighty word that saves to the uttermost. Only four per cent of the working classes attend a place of worship in London."

In a district in Norwich three fourths of the adult population are regular absentees from a place of worship. Out of 22,000 souls not more than 1,700 can read, including children. Here a woman of seventy was made a believer, not having previously known that there was a God, and a woman of forty thought that she "once heard something" about Jesus Christ, and asked, "Was He not the Son of the Saviour?" (p. 233.) No wonder that of the 320 prisoners in the county goal, the greater part are as ignorant as Hottentots. (p. 234.)

Though Dr. Shaw descants on the inferior physical development of the lower classes, still he observed "among the poor occasionally some of the highest forms of beauty living in pigstyes, ignorant as Hottentots, whose intellectual culture would stand on a par only with the instinct of brutes. They are angels in form, brutified and debased, living after the fashion of fleshy devils." (p. 270.)

Those who boast of the improvements, evidenced by the railways, electric telegraphs, philanthropic movements, &c., are asked by Dr. Shaw, have they made the morals better? He alludes to the wife-beating, murders without end, stabbing, the false marks of trade, adulteration of food, and, in the latter case, contrasts the "sacred liberty" of England with the preventive measures adopted in France against the poisoning of the supports of life. He quotes from one of the *Reviews*, that the concurrent opinion of men in business is that "the scrupulously honest man must go to the wall." (pp. 318, 314.) In such a state of things, and among such people, it is not surprising that the word of God, if honestly preached, should be ever offensive. But the Doctor asks, "Has it been so preached?" and answers, "I think not, save in a few instances. Our preachers, in a majority of cases, have been far too smooth—they have not preached against the vices of the age—they have been afraid of offending their congregations." (p. 320.) I wish this smoothness of preaching against *vice* would be adopted in preaching against Roman Catholic *belief.*

Dr. Shaw quotes from *The Literary Churchman:*—" It seems as if a reaction of unbelief were setting in, and as if we should ere long be placed face to face, more directly than ever, with the Anti-christ that denies that Jesus is the Son of God." So the eyes of sincere Anglicans are beginning to be opened, and the accursed deceiver is at length to be looked for nearer home than in the palace of the Vatican. Dr. Shaw adds, that "the Established Church at the present time, among some of its leading divines, appears to be not only schismatic to a very high degree, but marching on the highway, at a rapid rate, to a fearful state of heterodoxy." (p. 345.) He charges the Church with being asleep, in not attacking the sins of the age; in forgetting to whisper the law and the Gospel into the ears of hypocrites, and affirms that ninety-nine out of every hundred Christians do not believe in a Personal Advent. (p. 348.)

I may add that some of the individual cases of ignorance and infidelity, instanced by Dr. Shaw, are quite horrifying to read.

The Compass of March 9, 1861, after alluding to the "diametrically opposite opinions, of at least three great parties among the clergy" and "motley priesthood of the Church of England," asks, if it is to behold at length "some hopeful measures to prevent the national Church from being a mere Pantheon of tolerated opinions, in the widest and worst sense Catholic, by having ceased to be holy."

In the address of the Bishop of Winchester at a triennial visitation, reported in the *Record* of Oct. 22nd, 1862, he ascribed the paucity of candidates for Holy Orders, partly to "the diminution of *prizes*, as they were pecuniarily called, within the Church, consequent on the abolition of pluralities, and the reduction of cathedral establishments. ......There were, however, deeper causes," added his Lordship, "at work that tended to dry up the springs which had hitherto supplied the church with ministers, and which had not escaped the notice of an acute writer in a recent publication, who said that the strifes and dissensions, together with the scepticism disseminated by teachers within the church itself, had so perplexed the most earnest and acute of young minds that they dared not devote themselves to the ministry."

There is no mistaking the matter. Anglicanism, *as a religion*, is falling to pieces, the larger portions inclining variously toward

Infidelity, and the remainder toward old Catholicism. But the Establishment still appears secure, commanding the support of the aristocracy in the midst of its revenues and dignities; and its general popularity among a trafficking people must be expected to continue so long as its preferments may be disposed of by the hammer of the auctioneer. Alluding to this Evangelical trait, the *Times* of May 2, 1861, remarks that "there is nothing whatever to prevent any man from going to the *mart* and buying a living for his foolish, or fanatical, or profligate, or incapable son, and so setting him up as the lawful and spiritual medium between the Almighty and a thousand or two of His creatures;" and the *Dial* says in an article, headed "souls for sale," "The powers of endurance in certain points, possessed by the English people, are of all things to us most amazing; they let men be appointed to guide and guard their souls, by methods which they would not for a moment tolerate in the appointment of men to tend their cattle or to brush their boots."—(*Dial* of Jan. 25, 1861.) This refers particularly to the sale of the presentation to the living of Shelfanger, Norfolk, which was knocked down by auction in Garraway's Coffee House, on the 23rd. of January 1861, for the sum of £2,800.

It may not be out of place here to notice the means which are adopted for the defence of Anglicanism against infidelity. They often accord admirably with the eccentricities of its doctrines, and sometimes, in spite of the awfulness of the subject, almost excite our papistical laugh. Horsewhipping has been tried at Cambridge, where the presence of a Jew at dinner seems a cause for omitting the name of the Redeemer at grace. For such an "insult to his Lord and Saviour, Jesus Christ," one rev. gentleman admitted that he flogged another—a Fellow of Magdalen College. [See case tried before the University Court, reported in *The Times* of Feb. 4, 1861]. The Express (Daily News) of Dec. 3, 1860, gives us an account of a "Revival Meeting at Exeter Hall," where, after a prayer to the Almighty to stretch down His arm over London, for the purpose of converting it, and especially to check the growth of Popery, priestcraft, Puseyism, and devilism, a speaker addressed the meeting and assured them that the two classes most requiring conversion were the "working people, ninety-eight out of every hundred of whom never went to a place of worship at all, and the nobility, many of whom were canting humbugs." In such a state of religion he probably thought himself justified in calling churches with fine steeples, crosses, and "*fellows with white nightgowns on*," "miserable delusions." Another speaker followed, commencing with a hymn to the tune of "*The King of the Cannibul*

Islands," the auditory joining in chorus with the words " *Still I have no union.*" The speaker denounced the unconverted who believed that the *great scheme of human redemption was moonshine and humbug.* Desperate diseases require desperate remedies, and for many, even of his listeners, the preacher would prescribe " *shaking over Hell for five or six minutes,*" naively adding that "if that would not convert them nothing would." As he " warmed with his subject, he danced up and down the platform and shouted hell and damna- tion with a vigour which was perfectly appalling." During the proceedings, several young women *revived,* that is, *fainted ;* and we are not informed whether the results of the meeting were considered satisfactory, when on the *power of Christ to save being put to the vote,* the affirmative was carried by about three fourths of the audience holding up their hands.

Of a milder character than horsewhipping or " *shaking over hell*" *revivals,* but scarce less provocative of a popish smile, is the rather original plan noticed in the *Morning Herald,* under the head of " *New scheme for evangelizing London.*" The *Herald* says—

" An institution has been formed under the auspices of Lord Congleton, the Hon. and Rev. Baptist Noel, Mr. Scott (the Chamberlain of London), Dr. Forbes Winslow, and other gentlemen, for diffusing evangelical principles over the metropolis. To carry out their object, two large carriages have been constructed, which will be driven about London, stocked with Bibles, and accompanied by two men, one to propel and attend to the carriage and stock, the other to read in a clear loud voice such striking portions of the Scripture as would be likely to have an immediate and permanent effect upon the persons listening to them. It is contemplated to add to the number of the carriages until every district of London and its suburbs is compassed."

Gentlemen of " *The Irish Church Missions,*" listen ! We, Irish Catholics, believe in God, in Christ—in the Bible. In our communion are no infidels, no Neologians, no writers against any of the truths of revealed religion. We are, in fine, Christians, and are firm in our Christianity. In God's name, permit us to remain so undisturbed. Cease plying us with your tracts, your exterminations, your preachings, and your pistols. Turn your holy ardor to the preservation of your own Church, and try to rescue it from the infidelity into which the greater part of it is now so visibly merging. Go, Reverend Sirs, to England, and make an effort there to retain the thousands who are falling away from belief in Christ, and to gain the millions who have never risen to it.

NOTE C.

The following extracts, taken from the *Appeal to the Women of the United Kingdom*, by a committee of ladies, will suffice to show how the admirable *energy* of pious England makes its money in the factories. The Appeal is dated March 17, 1860.—

" FELLOW-COUNTRYWOMEN—Your voices are wanted — wanted throughout the kingdom—and wanted at once. Read the following. Our extracts are taken almost at random from ' Wrongs which cry for redress :'—*

" ' Samuel Price, examined — [examined, that is, by the Queen's Commissioner appointed to inquire into these atrocities. Reader, bear in mind that these statistics are recent, that these heart-sickening cruelties are going on now]—

" ' Samuel Price, examined—I was in the employment of Messrs. Ainsworth, near Bolton. They employ about four hundred people. It was mostly from eleven till two o'clock in the morning before we got off. In the last year I was with them, from April 1853 to April 1854; we were busy, as well as I can remember, through the spring and through the summer, for six or eight months of the year; that is, we went to work from six to half-past, sometimes at four, and left off from ten to twelve, one or two in the morning—and sometimes after that time....All the people 'in the works (females as well as males ; the young as well as adults) averaged this number of hours —some even more.'

" [Observe that this dreadful toil is not an occasional or exceptional fact. Girls and boys were thus working ' through the spring and through the summer, for six or eight months of the year.']

" ' At times, if a sudden order has come, we have not been in bed more than sixteen or eighteen hours in the week' averaging more than twenty-one hours and a half of unrest out of the twenty-four during seven successive days and nights for girls and boys, some of them no more than twelve years old.—Report of the Commissioner appointed to inquire how far it may be advisable to extend the provisions of the Acts for the better regulation of Mills and Factories to Bleaching Works, pp. 10, 11, Nos. 81-84.

" ' James Thompson (Mr. Wallace's Bleaching, Scouring, and Finishing Works for Cotton and Woollens, Burnbank, Glasgow).—I am manager to these works, and nephew of the owner. We employ about ten men and forty females....In summer some of the hands

* " *Houlston and Wright, London*, price 6d. Let those who peruse these ' Wrongs' take careful note of the ' REQUEST' at p. v."

work occasionally from 6 a.m. to 12 p.m. (eighteen hours) the whole week through : we did this last summer several times. Three days we worked twenty hours each day. The ages of most of our girls is from ten to eighteen.' (Mothers, observe these ages—some of the girls mere children). 'The stoverooms in which they work are in winter heated up to a 100° or 110° ; in summer the heat is from 120° to 130° (and at times very much higher, as stated by the same witness in evidence given at a subsequent examination). 'I feel, when I am urging the females to work these long hours, that I am doing what is not right, but I have been urged to do it to get a lot of goods finished. Sometimes they stay here all night, and then we make a place for them to lie down upon in a storeroom upon the pieces of goods unfinished. Sometimes fourteen or more girls will pass the night in this manner, after working nineteen hours, and coming out of those hot places dripping wet with perspiration, *and their clothes wet through with it.*'—*Ibid,* p. 59, Nos. 643, 645.

" And this in the country which is energizing through the world to put down slavery !

" ' Alexander King—I work at Mr. James Young and Son's bleach-works, Auldhousefield, Pollockshaw. There are about three hundred hands employed ; of these, two hundred and fifty are females. When we are busy the number is about four hundred....Sometimes, about once a week, one shift will begin at 6 a. m., and go on till six next morning (twenty-four hours). This has happened once a week on an average for the last six months. The females all work in the stoves.'—*Ibid,* p. 61, Nos. 682, 683.

" Alas, alas ! what a spectacle—what a hideous sickening spectacle —must these four hundred workers present at the close of their twenty-four hours' toil ! 'The females all work in the stoves !' Among them ' will be some from ten, eleven, to thirteen years of age ; the rest chiefly between that and twenty'—working twenty-four consecutive hours in places where the floors are stated by witnesses to be at times so hot that they burn the feet of those who tread on them !'—(*Minutes of Evidence,* Nos. 3,505—3,510.)

" ' Amelia Wood (fifteen next July).—I have been at this work about three years. We oftenest begin at five or six in the morning, and oftenest leave off at eleven or twelve   *   *   *   Sometimes we do not leave off till three or four in the morning. My fingers are often very bad—the cloth wears them through.'—*Ibid,* No. 158.

" Such is the every day complaint of suffering multitudes :—

" ' The friction of the piece, in hooking, cuts their fingers, and makes them very sore, their skins being soft. ' Whose finger is bleeding?' is not an uncommon expression, as the blood stains the pieces; they then have to have their fingers tied up.'—*Ibid*, p. 43, No. 414.

" As the blood stains the pieces!

" ' My feet are almost always sore.' (No. 226.) ' Have had the aching legs many a time.' (No. 228.)—' Ankle bone was growing out.' (No. 273.)—'The skin comes off, and they are very sore.' (No. 274.)—' I have often sore feet; they bleed sometimes, and my ankle bone has been growing out.' (No. 277.)—' The skin is off very often, and the soles of my feet are blood-raw.' (No. 279.)—' My feet are often blood-raw,'—' are often blood-raw, and they pain me.' (No. 281.)—' My feet blister at bottom, and are very sore. Mother puts some stuff to them that makes the new skin come.' (No. 285.)—' I have always sore feet in summer time.' (No. 533.)—' My feet are often sore winter and summer.' (No. 536.)—' Feet often so sore that the skin comes off with my stockings.' (No. 504.)—' If you could have seen my feet last night.' (No. 491.)—'Worked when the skin was off my feet very badly.' (No. 492.)—' I have often had the skin off my feet.' (No. 232.)—'Her feet very often get raw.' (No. 448.)— ' My feet were always sore in summer : they were blood-raw at bottom, and my ankles are swelled, with a deal of pain.' (No. 463.)

" Equally painful to contemplate is the ' dead-beaten ' state of the workers :—

" ' I have scores of times seen both men and children asleep at their work, and very dangerous work too.' (No. 10.)—' Very often they go to sleep over their work.' (No. 51.)—' I have had almost every day to take a board and beat it on the table to waken them, as they were slumbering at their work.'

" Samuel Price, examined before a select committee of the House of Commons (1857.)—Mr. Butt.—' How did you awaken them ? (alluding to the little children who fall asleep standing at their work) —'Many a time by shouting, and at other times getting a board and rapping it on the table, making a loud report that used to startle them, and I could keep them awake then for an hour, or more than that, perhaps, by frightening them.'—*Minutes of Evidence*, No. 1849.

" And this is England !"

" And this is England !" exclaim those worthy ladies. Yes ! and the England that mourns over the barbarism of Irish Popery ; and with money thus made she subscribes for our moral enlightenment !

NOTE D.

The following extracts from *My Diary in India*, by W. H. Russell,'
the celebrated *Times'* correspondent, will show the spirit in which
the war was carried on against the *rebel niggers* after A DAY OF
HUMILIATION :—" After the fusileers had got to the gateway, a Cash-
mere boy came towards the post, leading a blind and aged man, and,
throwing himself at the feet of an officer, asked for protection. That
officer, as I was informed by his comrades, drew his revolver, and
snapped it at the wretched supplicant's head. The men cried shame
on him. Again he pulled the trigger—again the cap missed—again
he pulled, and once more the weapon refused its task. The fourth
time—thrice had he time to relent—the gallant officer succeeded,
and the boy's life-blood flowed at his feet." (Vol. i. p. 348.) This
was not a bad specimen of England's pious bravery, but here is one
still better:—" Some of the Sepoys were still alive, and they were
mercifully killed, but for some reason or other that could not be explained, one of their number was dragged out to the sandy plain outside the house, he was pulled by the legs to a convenient place,
where he was held down, pricked in the face and body by the bayonets
of some of the soldiery, whilst others collected fuel for a small pyre,
and when all was ready, the man was roasted alive." It appears that
our Sikh troops were the actors in this scene, but "there were
Englishmen looking on—more than one officer saw it. No one offered to interfere!" The wretch attempted to escape, and leaped
away with the flesh hanging from his bones, but he was caught,
brought back and held on the fire with bayonets till his remains
were consumed. Mr. Russell's informant, who witnessed the scene,
excused his non-interference, saying that he could do nothing, as
the Sikhs were furious, and "*our own men encouraged them.*" (pp. 301,
302.) Speaking of a wounded child, who was lying with a parroquet
in a cage beside him, the bird screaming as if he knew what had
happened, he exclaims—" It is horrible, but it is true, that our men
have got a habit of putting natives out of pain as if they were animals. They do it sometimes out of charity." (p. 319.) He tells us
of a rebel whose life Captain Carey, on Walpole's staff, promised
should be spared, if he surrendered or "came in," and, when he
accordingly did so, he was seized by one Mr. Money, and hanged,
"loudly invoking with his last breath the honour of British officers
and the promise made to him." (p. 398.) Alluding to the Sepoy.
cruelties at Futtehguhr, Mr. Russell remarks that they were the acts
of barbarous savages ; but he asks, " Were our acts those of civilized
Christians, when at this very place we hung a relative of the Nuwab

of Furruckabad, under circumstances of the most disgusting indignity, whilst a chaplain," [a chief humiliator] " stood by among the spectators?" It appears the unfortunate man had declared his innocence of rebellion, and was satisfied that his statements were received, when two British officers, one of them a colonel, dined with him as his guests, a few hours before he was seized and hanged in some barbarous way, which Mr. Russell does not describe, but he affirms that " all these kinds of vindictive, unchristian, Indian torture, such as sewing Mahommedans in pig-skins, smearing them with pork-fat before execution, and burning their bodies, and forcing Hindoos to defile themselves, are disgraceful, and ultimately recoil on ourselves. They are spiritual and mental tortures, to which we have no right to resort, and which we dare not perpetrate in the face of Europe." (Vol. ii. pp. 42, 43.) Again, " one of the civilians of the station, who visited me, boasted that he had hanged fifty-four men in a few hours for plundering a village," and " he regretted that he had not more of it." *(Ibid,* p. 82.) Here, a second time, we are told the fate of prisoners that surrendered :—" They made signs to the officer that they would surrender, and he ordered them to come down the narrow staircase leading from the roof, and as the first Sepoy appeared, he told the man to take off his belt and pouch, and to lay it with his musket down upon the ground. The same thing he did with each, till he got them all, fifty-seven in number, upon which he said, ' I fell them in against the wall,' and told some Sikhs, who were handy, to polish them off! This they did immediately, shooting and bayoneting them," &c. *(Ibid.* pp. 295, 296.) Describing the seizure of Bene Madho's stronghold, Mr. Russell expresses his fears that " the cutting, and hacking, and bayoneting which went on was directed against *objects who were really not of a character to excite the animosity of an honourable enemy,* according to the laws of war." *(Ibid,* p. 331.) Who were the objects, Mr. Russell? Were they women and children, and prisoners? The truth is, I believe we had many a little Cawnpore of our own—and why not? Didn't we *humiliate* for it? But humiliated piety does not always kill : it is sometimes content with flogging; for instance, the army passed by a tomb at which a Moulvie was praying, when one of the officers proposed to destroy the tomb and to flog all the people who happened to be within reach." *(Ibid,* p. 342.) Such were the sequences of *Humiliation!* Such was the spirit in which the Gospel warriors of England carried on the war of retribution, and won the praises of their brethren in the Land of Bibles !

Mr. Russell speaks of the " *Ulster outbreak of* 1641." Did the massacres of the Papists in Island M'Ghee and other places occur

II

to him when he heard of the massacres by the column in advance of Havelock's force moving from Allahabad ? He was told by one of the officers that "the executions of natives in the line of march were indiscriminate in the last degree. In two days forty-two men were hanged on the road-side, and a batch of twelve men were exe-cuted *because their faces were turned the wrong way* when they were met on the march. These severities could not have been justified by the Cawnpore Massacre, because they took place *before* that diaboli-cal act." (Ib. p. 402). After this we are not surprised at the topes full] of rotting corpses which indicated the places where the special commissioners had been executing justice "an *in rei memoriam*," as Mr. Russell remarks, "*not apt to be speedily forgotten.*" (Vol. I. p. 214). I may here observe that, notwithstanding the reports so industriously propagated in England, it failed Mr. Russell in India to hear of a single lady who was mutilated by the Sepoys. (Ib. pp. 92, 117, 135, 136).

The antics and "*Mohawkery*" by which the intellectual young gentlemen, who officer our army, generally let off the exuberance of their spirits, together with the ferocity of the English in their treatment of Indians, their pretended religion and civilization ren-der them quite inscrutable beings to the Hindoo. Their popular character in India was described to Mr. Russell by a native gentleman, who said that the people looked on them very much as they would look on monkeys, but, at the same time " as some great powerful creatures sent to plague them, of whose motives and actions they can compre-hend nothing whatever." (Vol. II. pp. 145, 149) No wonder that the villagers, who came out "*with confidence* to look at the column," were those, many of whom "never saw a white face before in all their lives," and whose district was "rarely, if ever, visited by Euro-pean officials." (Ib. p. 349).

Few, I regret to state, take the trouble of investigating the beha-vior and policy of England in unfortunate India, though many books have been written on the subject; and among them I would recommend *Russell's Diary*; Ludlow's *The War in Oudh*; Norton's *Topics for Indian Statesmen*; Ludlow's *Thoughts on the Policy of the Crown towards India.*

The *Athenæum* newspaper, the clever opponent of prejudice, civil and religious, in its remarks on Mr. Ludlow's book, says :—"He shows that there was no chicanery to which recourse was not had to deprive the unfortunate natives of India of their rights. Starting with the insane notion that all land belonged to the British Govern-ment, and that it was desirable to reduce all princes, zemindárs, and wealthy proprietors to the uniform level of a pauper peasantry, the citizens of the old school inflicted injuries on India which it will take a century to remedy. We can only regret that such men should still have power to harm." I must specially recommend the admirable letter addressed to Count de Montalembert, by G. H. Moore Esq., late M. P. for Mayo. The older works, such as *Raynal's Indies*, may also be consulted with advantage.

NOTE E.

The claims of "the Establishment" to be called *a Church* in the Scriptural sense, may be well inferred from the following article abridged from *The Times* newspaper of January 26, 1856:—"We should think that no single column in our paper ever comprehended so great a variety of ideas, of institutions, and of modes of action and thought of professions, as the report that appeared on Friday of a hearing in the Court of Queen's Bench, headed ' The Queen v. the Archbishop of Canterbury.' Seldom have we felt so utter a sense of the hopeless entanglement in which Church and State have involved one another as on rising from the perusal of that column. Here is the case, if indeed it is possible to state a case which seems to elude the grasp of lawyers, divines, and everybody who tries to handle it: —It appears that two or three years ago Archdeacon Denison preached or published a sermon containing a certain sacramental theory, founded, we believe, on the literal sense of the words of institution. The Archdeacon intended his sermon to be a sort of defiance, and when a Mr. Ditcher took up the gauntlet he only did what the Archdeacon intended him to do. Mr. Ditcher proceeded under a statute of the present reign, complained to the Bishop of the diocese, and demanded a commission of inquiry into the sermon. The Bishop was an aged man, a personal friend of the Archdeacon, and very much of his opinion. So he did nothing, and nobody disputes his discretion in doing so. Another Bishop came to the see, and Mr. Ditcher, nothing daunted, renewed his complaint; or demand, with the like ill success. Thereupon, as the statute allowed him, he made the like complaint or demand to the Archbishop of the province. Here, at first, he was more successful. The primate appointed a commission of inquiry, but afterwards repented of his temerity, and resolved, if he could, to follow the example of the two bishops, and move no further in the affair.

When our readers have carefully and dispassionately considered the prospect that lay before the Archbishop, they will not be at all surprised at his change of purpose. The computation was, that the trial would cost the Archbishop a month of his precious time, and

10,000*l.* of his comparatively worthless money ; *that it was quite a toss up what the decision might be ;* that meanwhile there would be an immense deal of inquiry, and preaching, and testifying on a point which really defies human scrutiny, and the arguments of the Court would be echoed Sunday after Sunday from every pulpit in these isles ; that, supposing a judgment in favour of the Archdeacon, there would be an immense encouragement to mystical inquirers, not to say worse ; and, in the event of a judgment against the Archdeacon, an appeal to the Privy Council, and all the work, all the fuss, all the scandal to be undergone over again. The Archbishop could hardly reckon on seeing the end of the cause. It was quite certain that the judgment could not be of the smallest value one way or another, for such is the matter of the question, such the constitution of men's minds, and such is the latitude allowed by the formularies of our Church, that there will be differences on this question as long as our Church is a Church—one side taking the literal, the other the figurative, signification of Scripture.

The odd thing is, that this confusion, this uncertainty, this diversity of action between Bishops and Archbishops, these doubts as to the discretionary powers allowed by the act, these means of delay, which have already lengthened out the question from one Bishop to another, and may very possibly send it from one Archbishop to another,—this constitution of a court which the Archbishop himself declares to be incapable of commanding respect,— this series of appeals from the discretion of one Bishop to the discretion of another, thence to the indiscretion of an Archbishop, to a commission of inquiry, to a trial before the Archbishop, and thence to the Privy Council ; and, finally, this ruinous expense, are not the result of any old laws, but of an act passed in the present reign. What are we to say to this ? Shall we ask for some reform ? How do we know that it will be better than the last ? But it certainly does appear that in the present state of the law—and it was much the same in the old state—Bishops and Archbishops perform a very insignificant part in the government of the Church and the vindication of its doctrine."

This is the Church to which we are so " affectionately invited" to fly from the errors of Rome !

ADDITION TO NOTE 44.

I have tried to show the impossibility of being perfect in the faith that, excluding the interference of the Church, would receive the Bible as its sole Rule ; but we ought never to lose sight of the fact, that this wonderful Anglicanism, which proclaims liberation from

Church authority, at the same time imposes it. The Anglican may rejoice in his Bible Rule and the exercise of his private judgment, yet he becomes a heretic if he deviates from the Formularies of his Church; and by *these* it is, and *not by the Bible*, that heresy is to be determined. This dogma was well defined by the *Court of Arches* in the cases of two of the Reverend authors of the *Essays and Reviews*. According to Dr. Lushington's decision of June 25, 1862, it is manifest that in every point of doctrine comprised by the Liturgy and the thirty-nine Articles, the Anglican is as completely debarred as the Catholic from any right to interpret scripture for himself. If he disputes the Articles he is a heretic, for he denies the *infallible interpretation of his Church;* and still the Bible, we are gravely assured, examined by his private judgment, is his SOLE RULE OF FAITH!

Studying the contradictions of Anglicanism is a painful exercise of the mind; and it will be no small relief to the bewildered inquirer if he can find a point of its doctrine not involved in opposing theories. It appears, indeed, that the Anglican, who discusses any tenet not fixed by the Articles or the Liturgy, sins against no scheme of his religion when he regards the Bible as a legitimate field for the exercise of his judgment or his fancy. Here, in its mere enunciation, the doctrine of Private Judgment comprehends no inconsistencies, but then, among its results are some of the most remarkable that ever surprised the understanding or shocked the faith of a Christian. Witness the case of Dr. Rowland Williams, whose rejection of the Messianic prophecies was pronounced free from the guilt of heresy. "*Though I think,*" said the judge of the Court of Arches, "*that Dr. Williams's opinion militates against one of the most important doctrines held by the most venerated divines of the Church, I cannot come to the conclusion that the Articles of Religion or the Liturgy have in this respect been violated.*" So you may deny that the Messiah was foretold by the prophets. You may deny *His own words*, saying that He was, and yet you may be a true minister of the Anglican Church, justified by your right of private judgment in interpreting the Scriptures. What must we think of the *Rule of Faith* that leads to this? What must we think of the Church that admits it?

Following in the train of the *Essays and Reviews*, and with the additional eclat of episcopal authority, comes Dr. Colenso's work impugning the inspiration of the Pentateuch. Dr. Colenso, like a true Reformer, thus asserts his right to criticise the Scriptures:— "but, meanwhile, I cannot but believe that our Church, representing, as it is supposed to do, the religious feeling of a free Protestant nation, requires us now, as in the days of the Reformation, to protest against all perversion of the truth and all suppression of it for the sake of peace, or by mere authority." (Pref. p. xxxiii.) He quotes from *Bishop Butler*, who observes that "the Scripture-history *in general* is to be admitted as an authentic genuine history, *till* something positive be alleged sufficient to invalidate it" (p. 16), and the result of Bishop Colenso's examination of the Pentateuch is—"that the narrative, whatever may be its value and meaning, cannot be regarded as historically true" (pref. p. xx.) and "cannot possibly have been written by Moses or by any one personally acquainted with the facts which it professes to describe" (p. 8), and Dr. Colenso says:—"I cannot as a true man shut my eyes to the absolute, palpable, self-contradictions of the narrative." (p. 10.) But the Bishop still believes that the Pentateuch imparts "revelations of the Divine Will and Character" and probably, is quite right in remarking:—"*I am not aware of any breach of the law of the Church of England, as declared by the recent judgment in the Court of Arches, which is involved in this publication.*" (Pref. p. xxxiii.) Nor does he seem to rest satisfied with his criticisms on the Old Scriptures, for he says:—"Should God in His Providence call me to the work, I shall not shrink from the duty of examining on behalf of others into the question, in what way the interpretation of the *New* Testament is affected by the unhistorical character of the Pentateuch" (Pref. p. xxix.), and, bearing in mind the judgment to which he refers, it is hard to say how far he might not venture in denying the credibility of the Gospels without violating the law of the English Church.

Is it not, really, time for Anglicans to seek a *new* RULE OF FAITH for themselves rather than be troubled about the "errors" of Catholics? Is it not time for them to cease dinning our ears with a meaningless cant and to stop their loud trumpeting of Chillingworth's boast, that "the Bible, and the Bible only is the religion of Protestants?"

PRINTED BY RICHARDSON AND SON, DERBY.